BASICS
FASHION DESIGN
10

JEWELLERY
DESIGN

Ethical: aware-
ness/
reflect-
ion/
debate

ava
academia

An AVA Book

Published by AVA Publishing SA
Rue des Fontenailles 16
Case Postale
1000 Lausanne 6
Switzerland
Tel: +41 786 005 109
Email: enquiries@avabooks.com

Distributed by Thames & Hudson (ex-North America)
181a High Holborn
London WC1V 7QX
United Kingdom
Tel: +44 20 7845 5000
Fax: +44 20 7845 5055
Email: sales@thameshudson.co.uk
www.thamesandhudson.com

Distributed in the USA & Canada by:
Ingram Publisher Services Inc.
1 Ingram Blvd.
La Vergne TN 37086
USA
Tel: +1 866 400 5351
Fax: +1 800 838 1149
Email: customer.service@ingrampublisherservices.com

English Language Support Office
AVA Publishing (UK) Ltd.
Tel: +44 1903 204 455
Email: enquiries@avabooks.com

ISBN 978-2-940411-94-8

Library of Congress Cataloging-in-Publication Data
Galton, Elizabeth.
Basics Fashion Design 10: Jewellery Design / Elizabeth Galton p. cm.
Includes bibliographical references and index.
ISBN: 9782940411948 (pbk.:alk.paper)
eISBN: 9782940447213
1. Jewellery making. 2. Jewellery making -- Study and teaching. 3. Jewellery -- Design.
NK7304 .G357 2012

10 9 8 7 6 5 4 3 2 1

Design by Luke and Becky Herriott/www.studioink.co.uk

Cover: 'Castle opening drawbridge' ring in 18ct yellow gold and black diamond designed by Theo Fennell.

Production by AVA Book Production Pte. Ltd., Singapore
Tel: +65 6334 8173
Fax: +65 6259 9830
Email: production@avabooks.com.sg

Amanita Satana Diabolus necklace made with lacquered silver, bezel-set emeralds, and fluorescent lacquer with folds, designed by Victoire de Castellane.

Jewellery Design

Contents

The role of the jewellery designer is to create jewellery that is both visually appealing and highly wearable. A successful design concept challenges tradition or subverts the acceptable; it has the power to inspire reinterpretation and this in turn leads to ground-breaking movements, fashions and trends.

The jewellery designer's creative universe is limitless, informed by an endless stream of ideas, themes, motifs and historical references. Most jewellery designers' ideas evolve from a similar starting point, whether they are an independent jewellery designer or are employed by a brand.

This book explores the history of jewellery and the fine, couture and fashion jewellery markets, as well as topics such as ethical practice and marketing. It investigates the design process, how this evolves from an initial sketch to samples and then to the building of a collection. It looks at dealing with customers, press and buyers. It examines pricing, manufacturing and retailing.

The book also looks at the day-to-day life of a cross section of jewellery designers and the diverse set of skills required; from working on design collaborations to being a member of a design team. It provides an overview of the varied career paths and a window into the worlds of some of the most talented jewellery designers working today.

Intended to appeal to undergraduates, graduates, new professionals and jewellery enthusiasts, this book is underpinned by exclusive interviews from acclaimed designers and illustrated with dynamic images of outstanding jewellery. *Basics Fashion Design 10: Jewellery Design* is a rich source of inspiration and an essential tool for anyone considering a career in jewellery.

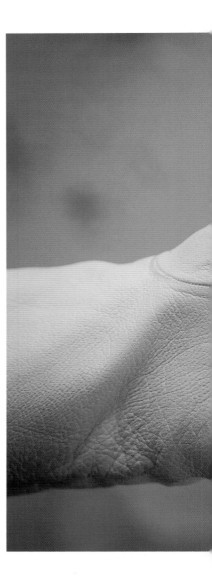

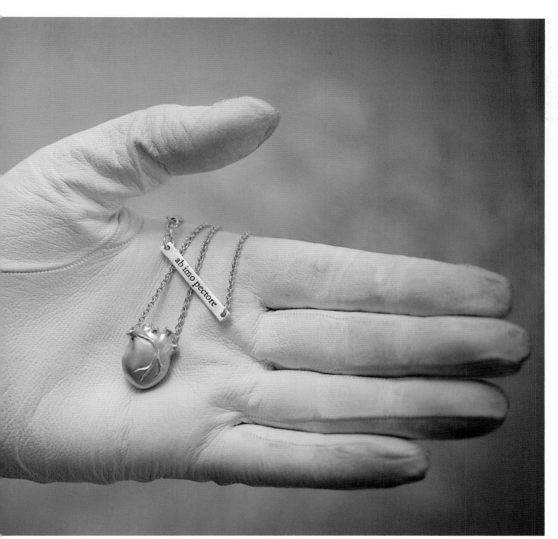

Heart necklace designed by Bjørg.
The message embossed on this
necklace paired with the motif of
the human heart captures the
magical symbolism of jewellery.

Introduction

John Galliano's Egyptian-inspired
jewellery for Christian Dior:
historical and cultural references
are a rich source of design
inspiration and have long been
plundered by jewellery designers.

Jewellery is an intensely personal art form, it is worn to look appealing, to enhance and decorate the wearer. It allows the wearer an opportunity to celebrate an occasion or key moment in life and encapsulates the spirit of an emotion forever. Throughout the ages, people have worn jewellery to connote status and wealth. Jewellery has the ability to cross genders, race and ages and appeals to that most human of emotions, namely, love.

The term 'jewellery' derives from the word 'jewel', which was anglicized from the old French *jouel* and before that, the Latin word *jocale*, literally meaning 'plaything'.

1. The unique patterns and style of Aztec gold jewellery have left a lasting impression on the jewellers of today.

2. The Ancient Egyptians had access to gold from which they made amulets, collars and diadems adorned with scarabs, birds and orbs, using lapis lazuli, turquoise and carnelian.

3. Maasai neckwear: the Maasai people come from East Africa and are famous for their beaded jewellery.

4. John Galliano's Maasai-inspired collection for Christian Dior.

1

2

This chapter looks at the long history of jewellery, from its origins to the innovations in the twentieth and twenty-first centuries. It explores how the past has influenced the present.

Jewellery has evolved over the centuries, from simple adornment made from shells, animal teeth, hair, berries and seeds worn both as talismans and as adornment. The oldest known pieces of jewellery are believed to be shells made into a necklace and found in Africa. The first signs of what we consider to be established jewellery making began in Ancient Egypt some 3,000–5,000 years ago and used materials such as vitreous enamel and glass.

Asia, and in particular the Indian subcontinent, has the greatest legacy of jewellery making, with a history spanning over 5,000 years. Jewellery making also developed in the Americas 5,000 years ago and in Central and South America; the Aztecs, Mayan and other Andean cultures are renowned for detailed gold jewellery.

In Africa, the Maasai are one of the most decorated people, known for their beaded jewellery, which is an important aspect of their culture. Throughout the world, ethnic groups are characterized and identified by dress and ornamentation.

3

4

Materials

Historically, jewellery has been made from a diverse range of materials, from textiles, beads, bone, glass and wood to plastics, precious and semi-precious stones, precious metals and found media. The processes and techniques for jewellery are ever evolving.

In many cultures jewellery is used as a means of storing wealth. Extreme articulation of the body has also been used to exaggerate the wearer's proportions. For example, the tribespeople of Papua New Guinea use feathers, pearl shells, wooden tallies and animal horns fashioned into ostentatious body adornment. The 'Giraffe' women of the Kayan tribe – situated between Burma and Thailand (also known as Padaung) – wear coiled neckwear that distorts the neck. The influence of this can be seen in the corset designed by Shaun Leane for Alexander McQueen's collection.

Tribal references have been plundered by designers for decades. It is an important skill to be able to reinterpret historical and cultural references in a contemporary way.

5

6

5. A woman from the Kayan tribe wearing coiled neckwear.

6. Horse hair necklace designed by Bjørg. By mixing craftsmanship, cultural and mythological references with more modern and urban concepts, designers speak of both the past and future.

7. Coiled corset designed by Shaun Leane for Alexander McQueen. (Autumn/Winter 1999).

7

Jewellery and fantasy

Jewellery has long held esoteric or religious association. For example, talismans and amulets, such as the 'evil eye', devotional medals and icons, such as the 'Hand of Fatima', are made from precious metals and gemstones and they are believed in some cultures to provide protection or ward off evil. Mystical and fantasy themes continue to inspire contemporary jewellers and the skull motif in particular is constantly celebrated.

9

8. The rose gold skull and crystal necklace, created by Indian-born designer Mawi Keivom, fuses contemporary style with traditional influences for an eclectic edge.

9. The skull is a popular motif for jewellery as shown in these skull cufflinks with articulated jaws from Deakin & Francis.

8

10

11

10. The 'Magik' wand pendant made with 18ct rose gold and natural cognac diamonds. Designed by Ana de Costa it reflects notions of symbolism and mysticism.

11. 'Evil eye' art pendant made with 18ct white gold, sapphire, diamond and black diamond, designed by Theo Fennell. (See page 119 for more about white gold.)

Materials, metals and stones

Jewellery is created from a myriad of metals, materials and stones.

Materials include: glass, leather, plastics and suede.

Metals include: aluminium, brass, bronze, copper, gold, palladium, rhodium, stainless steel, sterling silver (also Britannia silver and fine silver), titanium, and vermeil.

Stones include: agate, amber, amethyst, aquamarine, bloodstone, carnelian, chalcedony, chrysoprase, citrine, coral, diamond, emerald, garnet, jade, jasper, lapis lazuli, malachite, moonstone, obsidian, onyx, opal, pearl, peridot, quartz, rose quartz, ruby, sapphire, smoky quartz, spinel, sunstone, tanzanite, tiger's eye, topaz, tourmaline, turquoise, and zircon.

The origins of jewellery > Jewellery through the ages

Jewellery has evolved through the centuries according to the social and economic factors of the time. As fashions change, jewellery designs have adapted and materials have been developed to reflect the mood and collective consciousness.

It is important to have a broad knowledge of how jewellery has evolved throughout history and its relationship with fashion and accessories. Designers creating innovative jewellery should be aware of what has gone before and how social and economic factors have influenced design and manufacture.

In Europe during the 14th–16th centuries, the Renaissance brought significant advancements to jewellery as increased exploration brought exposure to the art of other cultures and trading led to the greater use of a variety of gemstones.

12. Peter Carl Fabergé created exquisite, lavish and ingenious Easter eggs for the Russian Imperial Court.

13. People have been wearing mourning jewellery for hundreds of years; this gold ring, c. 1640, has a skull bezel and crossbones enamelled in white. The eyes and shoulders are set with diamonds, and the hoop is in the form of tied ribbons enamelled in black.

14. Gisèle Ganne's duo ring recalls a fondness for the Victorian tradition of wearing mourning jewellery and challenges the notion that beautiful things can only ever be celebratory.

15. Jacqueline Cullen's hand-carved bracelet is made from Whitby jet and set with 18ct gold granulation and champagne diamonds. This designer is giving jet jewellery a modern spin. Cullen has revived the use of Whitby jet, bringing a contemporary relevance to a historical subject.

12

13

1800s

When Napoleon Bonaparte was crowned Emperor of France in 1804, he revived the sense of grandeur of jewellery in France. Jewellers began to design suites of matching jewellery such as diamond earrings, rings, brooches, tiaras and necklaces. New jewellery terms were established to differentiate jewellers. Those working in cheaper materials were called *bijoutiers* and jewellers who worked with expensive materials were called *joailliers*; the distinction continues to this day in France.

Romanticism also defined the era, in keeping with the public's fascination for the treasures being unearthed through the birth of archaeology and a love of Renaissance art. This period saw the establishment of a number of famous jewellery houses, including Tiffany and Company, Fabergé and dynastic, Italian master jeweller Bulgari. During this period the most notable development was the birth of modern production methods.

In England in 1843, Garrard – the oldest fine jewellery house in the world (established in London in 1735) – was bestowed the honour of Crown Jeweller in 1843 by Queen Victoria and has since served six successive monarchies.

The Victorian period also saw an increase in the popularity of 'mourning jewellery' or 'memorial jewellery', after the death of Queen Victoria's consort Prince Albert in 1861. This type of jewellery was presented to the friends and families of the bereaved to commemorate the dead. This tradition prevailed for several hundred years and common symbols used in mourning jewellery included skulls, coffins and gravestones and often featured plaited hair of the deceased – hair, a symbol of life, has long been associated with death and funerals in many cultures.

During the Victorian era, the mourning motifs grew to include forget-me-nots, flowers, hearts, crosses, and ivy leaves. Whitby jet (a fossilized wood found only in Whitby, UK) became a popular material for such artefacts.

14

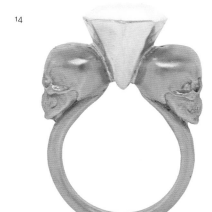

15

Art nouveau

The art nouveau movement (at its height between 1890–1910), was characterized by a soft, organic aesthetic and motifs such as flowers, birds and dragonflies. During this period, jewellers placed a distinct emphasis on colour achieved with the use of specialist enamelling techniques such as *cloisonné* and *plique-à-jour*.

René Lalique's revolutionary creations made him a master of the art nouveau style. Miniature sculptures in their own right, his signature motifs included mythical creatures, insects and exotic flowers and, audaciously for the time, he referenced the female form, as an allegory – half woman, half animal. Lalique explored previously unfashionable materials such as horn and ivory, combining them with semi-precious stones, glass, pearls and enamel.

At this time, Europeans began to develop a fascination with jewellery, prints, paintings, prose, photography and poetry influenced by Japan and known as *Japonisme*.

Cartier SA, established in 1904, was another highly influential jewellery house in the art nouveau movement. Cartier's clientele throughout the decades have included royalty and movie stars attracted by its finely crafted jewellery and watches.

16. The revolutionary creations of the jeweller René Lalique made him a master of the art nouveau style. Design of René Lalique 1897–98. Corsage ornament *Femme-libellule*.

(© Musée Calouste Gulbekian, Reinaldo Viegas, Lisbonne)

16

17. René Lalique drawing of a *Lorgnette Femme Ailé*.

(© Lalique)

18. Design of René Lalique 1897–98. Corsage ornament *Femme-libellule*.

(© Musée Calouste Gulbekian, Reinaldo Viegas, Lisbonne)

The Arts and Crafts Movement

The design philosophy of the Arts and Crafts Movement in England flourished circa 1880–1910. It was notable for its linear aesthetic. The movement originated as a reaction against the industrial revolution and mass manufacturing practices. It advocated a return to craftsmanship and creative independence. Its ideas spread throughout Europe and America.

The designer and writer William Morris and the theorist and critic John Ruskin were two of its most influential figures. Morris, famous for his pattern designs for textile and wallpaper, placed great value on craftsmanship and the natural beauty of materials. Ruskin was interested in the relationship between art and society.

By the 1880s, Morris had become an internationally renowned and commercially successful designer and manufacturer. New guilds and societies began to take up his ideas, presenting for the first time a unified approach among architects, painters, sculptors and designers. In doing so, they brought arts and crafts ideals to a wider public.

In the 1890s, Arthur Lasenby Liberty, the founder of the store Liberty London (UK), became interested in design from both the Arts and Crafts and art nouveau movements.

In 1899, the jewellery designer Archibald Knox began designing for Liberty, his work was influenced by the Arts and Craft Movement.

19

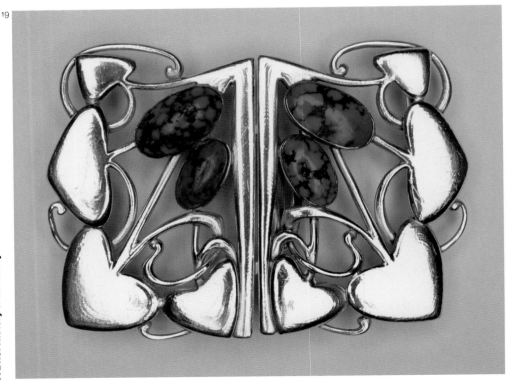

1920s

The economic and social pressures that immediately followed the First World War (1914–18) brought with them a new mood for a rigorous and clean-cut look. Art deco was an innovative design style popular in the 1920s during the era of the flapper, and the jazz and machine age. It was epitomized by streamlined forms and simple, abstract, geometric patterns and a strikingly graphic use of colours, particularly red, black and green. Influences included Egyptian pharaohs, the Orient, tribal Africa, and the art movements of cubism and futurism.

Art deco combined mass production with the sensitivity of art and design that had gone before. Fine jewellery names that typified the era include Cartier, Jean Després, Boucheron, Joseph Chaumet, Raymond Templier, Lacloche Frères and Vacheron Constantin.

19. Archibald Knox designs for Liberty were synonymous with the British Arts and Craft Movement.

20. Louise Brooks, the 1920s' silent film star, was notable for her look which featured boldly geometric jewellery styles and a particular fondness for Raymond Templier's designs.

21. Louise Brooks epitomized the era with her graphic bobbed hair and chic sautoir pearl necklace falling to the hips.

20

21

1930s

Costume or fashion jewellery became widely popular in the 1930s as a cheap, disposable accessory of a throwaway nature. It had no significant material value and was usually designed to complement a particular look.

Costume jewellery was made of inexpensive simulated gemstones, such as rhinestones or paste, and materials such as Lucite, pewter, silver, brass and nickel.

Visionary designer Coco Chanel popularized the use of 'faux' or 'costume jewellery' and created a one-off diamond collection inspired by stars and comets in 1932, which was revolutionary for post-Depression Paris.

22

22. Coco Chanel rose to become one of the premier fashion designers in Paris. Progressive for her time she replaced the corset with comfort and casual elegance, and championed the wearing of costume jewellery.

'A woman should mix fake and real. To ask a woman to wear real jewellery only is like asking her to cover herself with real flowers instead of flowery silk prints. She'd look faded in a few hours. I love fakes because I find such jewellery provocative, and I find it disgraceful to walk around with millions around your neck just because you're rich. The point of jewellery isn't to make a woman look rich but to adorn her; not the same thing.'
Coco Chanel

'Jewellery takes people's minds off your wrinkles!'
Elizabeth Taylor

1940s–50s

During the World War II era, sterling silver (see also page 121) was often incorporated into costume jewellery designs, since the components used for base metal were needed for wartime production and a ban was placed on their use in other areas.

The contemporary jewellery movement began in the late 1940s and coincided with a period of renewed interest in artistic and leisure pursuits. In the 1940s, designers merged natural materials with plastics and other modern materials such as Bakelite. This period was defined by a look that exuded glamour and motifs such as flowers, bows, sunburst designs, and ballerinas abounded.

In the 1950s, jewellery designs became more understated, in keeping with the tailored styles of the day, characterized by Dior's bold 'New Look'. Bold jewellery such as large, chunky bracelets and charm bracelets adorned with semi-precious stones such as jade, opal, citrine and topaz were popular.

23. Exquisitely crafted with signature wit, Theo Fennell's modern day 'Lips' charm is reminiscent of Schiaparelli's earlier lips brooch, designed for her by the surrealist artist Salvador Dali in 1949, and inspired by Mae West's come-hither smile.

24. A 'Tuileries' topaz jewellery set by Christian Dior consisting of a necklace, bracelet and head adornment from 1956.

25. Audrey Hepburn had an acclaimed and iconic style notable for its jewellery worn in films such as *Breakfast at Tiffany's* and *Funny Face*. Her style bridged the gap between the formality of the 1950s with the more relaxed 1960s.

The origins of jewellery > **Jewellery through the ages** > Interview: Anne Kazuro-Guionnet

1960s and 1970s

The contemporary jewellery movement of the period was spearheaded in the 1960s by pioneering American and European jewellery designers and broke new ground with the use of industrial metals such as aluminium and stainless steel. Acrylics such as Lucite and Perspex became popular in Pop Art style jewellery. The broadening range of plastic and printed nylons reflected a brave new world – a space age with new unexplored frontiers for mankind.

Designers such as Emmy van Leersum and Gijs Bakker championed the new era with work such as unisex metal body wear that celebrated the wearer's erogenous zones, which created a great deal of controversy. Designs had a distinctly 'space age' style. The modern, geometric shapes blurred the boundaries between art, fashion and jewellery, provoking interesting questions on jewellery in relation to status; replacing an emphasis on intrinsic value with one that placed an importance on the value of ideas.

Kenneth Jay Lane and Elsa Peretti, who joined Tiffany & Company in 1974, were notable American jewellery designers working within the environs of fashion during this time.

26

26. Emmy van Leersum in 1968 wearing an aluminium collar and dress of her own design. (Collection: Stedelijk Museum's Hertogenbosch)

27

27. Elsa Peretti's minimalist jewels with fluid lines and sensual forms caused a stir in the jewellery world, and her enduring motifs of the 1970s are still popular more than 30 years on.

The 1980s

Fashion became a more pivotal influence as costume jewellery was propelled forward by the maximalist baroque-styles and loud colours of fashion designers including Christian Lacroix, Versace and Karl Lagerfeld at Chanel, who revived and re-styled many of Chanel's concepts.

Entertainers and the increase popularity of music videos also drove jewellery trends. For example, some jewellery was heavily linked to the birth of American 'hip hop' culture. Pioneers of this music culture later coined the term 'bling bling' in reference to ostentatious displays of heavy gold jewellery worn by rap and hip hop stars with label-heavy clothes.

Jewellery has often been favoured as a means of expressing a person's affiliation with a particular group. In the 1970s–80s, the punk movement utilized body piercings, studs, chains and safety pins to create a provocative look, which was a reaction against the Establishment and a product of a newly recognized and influential youth culture. It is a theme that continues to inspire jewellers, fashion designers and youth cultures today.

28

28. Music was a pivotal influence on jewellery styles in the 1980s with stars such as Toyah Wilcox and Madonna mixing and layering glitzy jewellery styles.

29. Gisèle Ganne's divorce knuckleduster ring connotes notions of dead relationships and decaying marriages in our modern times.

The 1990s

In the 1990s the trend for more minimalist designers, such as Jil Sander, Donna Karan, Helmut Lang, Giorgio Armani and Calvin Klein, became popular and jewellery reflected the simplistic mood of the era. The overstated style and the ostentation of the 1980s was eschewed for a pared down and unadorned aesthetic and muted tones, favoured by style icons such as Carolyn Bessette Kennedy, teamed with simple basics such as a stud earring. Fine jewellery was the sole preserve of classical fine jewellery houses such as Harry Winston and Cartier.

In the late nineteenth century, the American jewellery industry began fostering the idea of wedding rings for both men and women. They encouraged the practice with tactical marketing campaigns and wedding rings for men gained significant momentum during the Second World War (1939–45). This has since expanded into a highly lucrative sector of the market and includes celebratory rings, pair rings (exchanged by lovers) and celebratory jewellery signifying love, partnerships and births.

Modern takes on the theme include Cartier's iconic 'Love' collection which is founded on the concept of a band of gold with gold screws, a modern interpretation of the unbreakable bonds of love.

One designer who has bucked the trend and created a novel spin on celebratory jewellery and cultural signifiers is Gisèle Ganne whose 'Divorce Ring' reflects our fractured times. Today, 42 per cent of marriages finish in divorce in the UK and 38 per cent in France. Gisèle Ganne's divorce jewellery refers to old and contemporary wedding customs. In France, a Bride Globe was presented to the bride in which to put her bouquet and her crown after the wedding. All the decorations inside symbolize the union and give luck to the marriage. Gisèle uses union and marriage symbols and subverts them to show the inevitability of a breakup, but also to show that from these ashes a new life may rise.

29

New techniques

The late twentieth century saw the blending of European design with oriental techniques such as *mokume gane* (a process that involves the fusing and laminating of layers of metal) as well as new processes such as anticlastic raising, where sheet metal is shaped by compressing its edges and stretching the centre. Other processes such as hydraulic die forming, fold forming, metal anodizing, photo etching and the use of CAD (computer-aided design) and CAM (computer-aided manufacturing) saw the boundaries of jewellery making expand still further.

Fashion became a dynamic force in the fine jewellery sector and branded jewellery per se has accelerated rapidly. Luxury conglomerates such as LVMH (who own Fred, Chaumet, De Beers, and Bulgari) and fashion mega brands such as Chanel, Dior, Hermès and Gucci have infiltrated the fine jewellery market, creating collections more in tune with contemporary lifestyles. Fine jewellery, once dominated by the classical jewellery houses, is enjoying a revival combining a modern flavour with timeless materials.

Polish designer Tomasz Donocik (UK Jewellery Designer of the Year 2011) is known for reinterpreting modernity through subverting motifs of classicism and masculinity. He creates collections driven by themes, the inspiration for which he draws from literature, culture and architecture. His designs are often bold and androgynous and exploit a range of materials challenging traditional ideas of accessorizing.

30. Tomasz Donocik designed these cuffs inspired by the Chesterfield sofa and club chairs associated with aristocrats during the nineteenth century. The quilted leather pattern combined with precious materials is luxurious and glamorous.

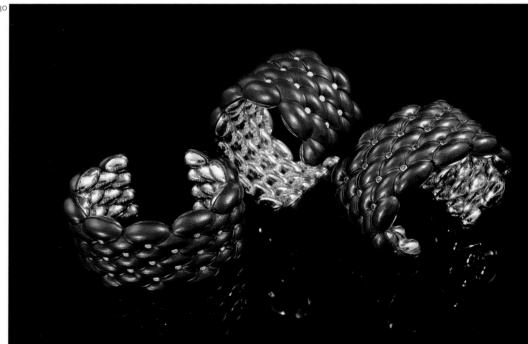

30

The future

31

As the twenty-first century advances, jewellery is embracing new technology, particularly computer-aided design (CAD), which is more usually associated with architectural design and the aviation sector. Traditional jewellery making is being juxtaposed with innovative production methods such as ultra-fine laser engraving and laser welding, which allow designers to create finer, more delicate creations. Techniques also include the development of new high-tech plastics, and laser and high-pressure water cutting techniques, CAD imaging and the evolution of new metal alloys, such as Tiffany's 'Rubedo' (which means 'redness' in Latin); a pinkish mixture of copper, silver and gold.

Advances in processes, such as the ability to laser engrave stones with words or messages invisible to the naked eye, are contributing to defining a new aesthetic that blends artisan techniques with high-tech methods, so that what was once a traditional craft industry is now moving with the times.

The use of materials such as titanium, which is stronger and lighter than steel, in jewellery is resulting in exciting, innovative designs previously almost impossible to conceive.

Innovative retail developments bring together the world of high tech and high jewellery. One of the leaders in 3D augmented reality (AR) is Holition, which uses it to add a new virtual dimension to online shopping.

This 3D digital experience allows online consumers to download software and cut out a paper marker of a product, this then allows them to virtually 'try on' and see themselves wearing the jewellery or watch by holding it up to their computer screen. This interactive element appeals to a tech-savvy digital audience and younger consumers.

31. Sarah Herriot's 18ct gold 'Twist and Shout' ring. Sarah's skill in employing cutting-edge 3D design technology results in a unique and distinctive architectural quality.

The origins of jewellery > Jewellery through the ages > Interview: Anne Kazuro-Guionnet

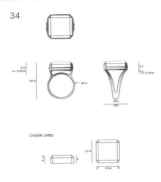

32. Anne Kazuro-Guionnet

33. Lalique *Aréthuse Révélation* ring in silver and clear crystal emerald cut, 2011 collection. (© Lalique)

34. Technical drawing for the *Aréthuse Révélation* ring. (© Lalique)

Anne Kazuro-Guionnet is head of jewellery at Lalique. René Lalique founded his eponymous brand in 1885, his art nouveau style transformed French jewellery from an industry into an art form in its own right. Lalique is renowned for its glass creations.

Lalique is a high-profile heritage house, how are you reinterpreting the design aesthetic?

I start with the Lalique DNA, the four sources of inspiration: sensual water, enchanting air, extravagant earth and charismatic fire. Once the story is defined for the year, we analyse the heritage jewellery drawings by René Lalique that best fit the story (patterns, volume, colours, and wear). We blend all these to reinvent the design aesthetics whilst respecting the Lalique style (from art nouveau to art deco).

How do you balance heritage with contemporary design?

To avoid just a re-run of the heritage and to achieve a good balance with contemporary design, you always have to keep in mind the following three building blocks.

1. Understand the sense of the heritage. From my point of view, the 'sense of the heritage' is based on an individual story, a unique style, specific patterns and different sources of inspiration.

2. Have an eclectic and international view of jewellery based on ethical habits, gemology expertise balanced with technical innovations and market statistics. From here, the contemporary vision can begin.

3. Be passionate about heritage and keep it alive for future generations.

How would you describe your design style?

It is built on four fundamentals: volume, contrasted shapes, contrasted textures and mix of materials.

35

36

37

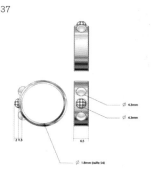

35. Inspiration for the *Pétillante* ring, an original Mossi vase by René Lalique, 1933. (© Lalique)

36. Lalique *Pétillante* ring in silver and clear crystal, 2011 collection. (© Lalique)

37. Technical drawing for Lalique *Pétillante* ring. (© Lalique)

How do you start your collections?

There are four points to the Lalique Joaillerie strategy.

1. Clean and build the collection.

2. Renew the collection, building three categories of products: the eye-catching pieces (the most daring and high-end positioning), the ceremonial designs (such as bridal or celebration products) and the bread and butter products.

3. To develop the collection, focusing on Limited Edition, market exclusivity increasingly adapted to our new audience, and creating desirable iconic designs.

4. To consolidate the collection, focusing on the sustainability of our designs.

Usually, the design process starts with the story of the year, referencing the archive designs, combined with a modern reinterpretation and following the strategic marketing plan and trends.

How many collections do you work on in a year?

We are working for the first season of the year to deliver the collection the following year, and the second season in order to deliver two years after that.

How is the design team structured?

The jewellery team is made up of a designer, a product manager, an operational marketing manager, a development and quality manager and myself.

What advice would you give to a young designer?

Have humility and always keep your five senses awakened.

What are your plans for the future?

Hopefully we will bring more obscure and interesting unseen historical garments into the spotlight and continue to make them in the most authentic way possible.

Researching and translating historical and cultural references is a vital part of design. Primary research should inform the starting point of any design and almost anything can inspire you. Visit galleries, museums, shops and markets and explore other cultures and modes of dress. Themes from film, history or literature are also a good reference point to spark ideas. Look at inspiring shop windows and visual merchandising displays of key brands that you admire.

38. Earrings designed by Leyla Abdollahi made with 18ct yellow gold with green amethysts, light blue sapphires and white sapphires. This design celebrates mythology and is inspired by the Okeanis eponym of Persia, who was loved by the sun god Helios.

38

■ The more diverse your research, the more likely you are to achieve a successful outcome.

■ Choose a key period in history or culture that appeals to you and immerse yourself in all aspects of it – this may include literature, art or architecture or the colours, styles, tribal dress or fashions.

■ From your research, build a scrapbook that includes photographs, references from books, materials, and text.

■ The objective is to build a visual library that informs your design work and helps you to begin building your own unique design signature.

■ Consider how you can manipulate or subvert your chosen historical or cultural reference; translating it in a contemporary way.

■ This could include incorporating an unexpected material or colour into a traditional motif, or objects associated with a particular period or culture. Explore new ways of approaching a traditional mode of dress or jewellery style to lend a sense of modernity and a element of the unexpected to the theme. The aim is to give your audience a sense of the original historical reference but at the same time offer a fresh, dynamic approach and a new perspective.

■ Next, look at particular groups such as the Edwardian dandies, hip hop, and punks, or tribal communities and street culture, such as Japanese 'Harajuku', from which new trends and distinct styles arise.

■ Consider and identify how these groups approach colour, texture and forms in terms of accessories, jewellery and clothing.

■ How do these choices accentuate or distort the human form? Are they provocative or wearable, exaggerated or understated?

39. Japanese girls wearing 'Harajuku' style street fashion. Youth culture remains a strong influence for designers looking to anticipate upcoming trends.

40. An oxidized silver signet ring from the 'Ivy Noir' collection designed by SMITH/GREY. This collection is a twist on the traditional Ivy League style interpreted with a dark edge.

'Belle a Lier' body jewellery designed
by Shaun Leane for Swarovski
Runway Rocks made with
Swarovski Elements.

Jewellery concerned with the fashion and lifestyle arena (as opposed to the craft or art jewellery movement) is made up of several key groups including fine jewellery, fashion jewellery and catwalk (runway) jewellery, each with a specific position in the market and customer demographic. Whilst designers may specialize in one area, they must have a good understanding of the market as a whole in order to be versatile and ensure a broad commercial portfolio.

A designer's creative signature may be translated to other product categories such as watches, sunglasses, leather goods, such as handbags and belts, and other accessories.

This chapter gives an introduction to the key jewellery categories as well as topics such as ethical practice and new technologies. As the book unfolds, it explores the knowledge you will need to acquire in order to create your own jewellery collections.

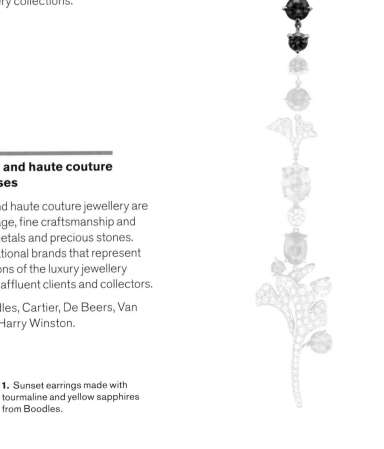

1

Fine jewellery and haute couture jewellery houses

Fine jewellery and haute couture jewellery are defined by heritage, fine craftsmanship and the use of rare metals and precious stones. These are aspirational brands that represent the upper echelons of the luxury jewellery market aimed at affluent clients and collectors.

Examples: Boodles, Cartier, De Beers, Van Cleef & Arpels, Harry Winston.

1. Sunset earrings made with tourmaline and yellow sapphires from Boodles.

Jewellery Styles

Mega brands

International fashion mega brands feature a broad portfolio of luxury products including accessories, fashion jewellery (and in some cases fine jewellery) and watch collections with a highly identifiable aesthetic featuring iconic motifs and logos and brand specific colours.

Examples: Gucci, Hermès, Louis Vuitton.

Mid-market brands

Mid-market brands sit between the mass market and the luxury market retailing via stand-alone stores, concessions within department stores and airports. The middle market comprises jewellery brands or fashion brands creating affordable collections of semi-precious jewellery and entry-level fine jewellery as part of a branded, retail experience and many have coined the term 'affordable luxury'.

Examples: Hot Diamonds, Links of London, Pandora.

Commercial market

Commercial fashion brands are usually sold on the high street. This is often off-the-shelf jewellery sourced directly from manufacturers or in-house designers who customize designs from a library of existing jewellery components. Products are heavily trend led, disposable and have a fast turnover.

Examples: Claire's Accessories, Folli Follie, Topshop.

Independents

Amongst these categories sit independent designers, who operate across these tiers depending on their price points and brand positioning. Retailing directly to customers and store buyers via trade shows, websites, multi-brand stores, online marketplaces and jewellery galleries, and in some cases standalone stores. This category may also include art jewellers more concerned with the conceptual and material specialisms.

Examples: Tom Binns, SMITH/GREY, Monica Vinader.

2

2. Golden horse hoop earrings from the 'I Can't Seem to Get Rid of the Horses' collection, designed by SMITH/GREY.

Jewellery categories > Catwalk jewellery

Catwalk jewellery comprises one-off jewellery showpieces designed primarily for the fashion catwalk (runway). It is a very specialized, intensely creative aspect of couture jewellery. These creations are not constrained by the usual commercial and practical considerations and provide an opportunity for designers to exercise creative free rein. They are an explosion of ideas that challenge traditional notions of what jewellery is and where and how it can be worn.

Inspirational designers and jewellers who create pieces that define the genre

Alexandra Byrne, Hussein Chalayan, Igor Chapurin, Erickson Beamon, Philippe Ferrandis, Zaha Hadid, Kirt Holmes, Christopher Kane, Shaun Leane, Julien Macdonald, Jenny Manik Mercian, Corto Moltedo, Nusch, Otazu, Johnny Rocket, Marios Schwab, and Lesley Vik Waddell.

3. 'Love Hurts' body wrap and crystallized bra designed by Johnny Rocket for Swarovski Runway Rocks made with Swarovski Elements.

4. 'Crystal Bubbles' headpiece designed by Naomi Filmer for Swarovski Runway Rocks made with Swarovski Elements.

3

4

5 Catwalk jewellery showpieces are extravagant and intended to garner press coverage; they are often the result of collaboration with a fashion designer who uses couture jewels as the finishing touches to a fashion catwalk presentation. Catwalk presentations convey a creative vision for the season and such *objets d'art* and haute couture fashion drive sales of mainline ready-to-wear collections and influence and filter down to the mainstream market.

Catwalk designs push the boundaries of scale, materials and proportion not usually suited to daily wear. They provide a cross fertilization of ideas with jewellery, adornment, fashion, art and sculpture, merging to create thought-provoking pieces. While not necessarily made from precious materials, these pieces will nevertheless have a conceptual value.

6 Swarovski's acclaimed *Swarovski Runway Rocks* features some of the most visionary catwalk jewels in the world from the most cutting-edge international design talent. The brand has a long tradition of collaborations with the fashion and jewellery industries and has developed its mastery of precision-cutting, to become the world's leading producer of cut crystal, genuine gemstones and created stones; these products have been the main component of Swarovski's catwalk jewellery.

5. 'Celeste' necklace and cuff designed by Zaha Hadid for Swarovski Runway Rocks made with Swarovski Gemstones.

6. 'Enchantment' neckpiece, designed by Lesley Vik Waddell for Swarovski Runway Rocks made with Swarovski Elements.

...haracterized by exclusive ...culate craftsmanship. ...ious metals and gemstones, they are enormously valuable and represent heirlooms of the future. Key centres of fine jewellery are Bond Street, London (UK) and the Place Vendôme, a seventeenth-century square in the first arrondissement of Paris (France). In the US, 5th Avenue in New York is home to many prestigious fine jewellery bands.

7

The most avant-garde creator of our times is *Haute Joaillerie* designer Victoire de Castellane for Dior Fine Jewellery. Responsible for some of the most staggeringly exuberant fine jewellery, her pieces are works of art. Characterized by a veritable kaleidoscope of candy colours and precious stones, she derives inspiration by mixing historical and contemporary sources.

7. 'Armour-dillo' ring made with 18ct white gold with black diamonds and emeralds from the 'Murder She Wrote' collection, designed by Stephen Webster.

Fine jewellery brands

8

Asprey, Boucheron, Bulgari, Cartier, Victoire de Castellane, Chanel Fine Jewellery, Chaumet, Chopard, De Beers, Fabergé, Theo Fennell, Garrard, Graff, H.Stern, JAR, Lalique, Shaun Leane, Mappin and Webb, Mauboussin, Mikimoto, Michelle Ong, Piaget, Ritz Fine Jewellery, Jean Schlumberger, Van Cleef & Arpels, Louis Vuitton Fine Jewellery, Stephen Webster, and Harry Winston.

8–9. Victoire de Castellane's jewellery is inspired by many references including the synthetic wonders of technicolour; characters from the Brothers Grimm fairy tales, Walt Disney and Japanese manga characters.

Jewellery Styles

9

Fashion jewellery is worn for its fashion or design content, which distils seasonal trends, textures and colours. Designers use a variety of materials, semi-precious gemstones and non-precious materials at prices more affordable than fine jewellery. Fashion jewellery is a fashion statement in its own right.

10. Vintage design leaf pendant with black onyx disc and blue apatite chain, designed by Denise Manning.

11. Atelier Swarovski necklace made with crystal by Mary Katrantzou.

12. Atelier Swarovski 'Bolster' bracelets in assorted colours by Christopher Kane.

Key fashion jewellers

Philippe Audibert, Aurélie Bidermann, Tom Binns, Burberry, Butler & Wilson, Erickson Beamon, Folli Follie, Lanvin, Marc Jacobs, Marni, Moschino, Mulberry, Prada, Yves Saint Laurent, and Swarovski.

11

Jewellery designers take their lead from fashion trend information and colour palettes and attention is paid to scale, texture, fastenings (findings and closures) and colour. Designs are diverse and include global, tribal, ethnic and street style references and motifs found in architecture, nature and found objects. There are a plethora of ideas saturating the market and the challenge is to arrive at the next bestselling product.

Jewellery is an important category in the fashion industry, it reflects how creativity, wearability and commerce can go hand in hand. By collaborating with a fashion brand or by working in a freelance capacity, a talented fashion jewellery and accessories designer can command considerable influence within the fashion world.

12

The cocktail ring

The cocktail ring became popular during the days of prohibition (1919–33) in the US at illicit cocktail parties and secret clubs, which were known as 'speakeasies'. Women used these social gatherings to dress up and show off their elaborate rings featuring a large central semi-precious stone or crystal.

Cocktail rings were made by both fine and fashion jewellery houses. After prohibition ended, cocktail rings continued to be in demand at cocktail parties popular during the 1940s and 1950s. Cocktail rings are also known today as statement rings, and are as popular now as when they first came into vogue.

13. Hedone Romane's 'Touch Me Not' cocktail ring in 18ct white gold with cushion-cut garnet centre, partly pavéd with rubies and white diamonds, is a surrealist interpretation of the enigmatic baccara rose.

13

14

Cufflinks

The forerunner of today's cufflinks appeared during the reign of Louis XIV when ruffled wristbands were finished with small openings on either side that tied together with cuff strings. Shirt sleeves began to be fastened with sleeve buttons, typically identical pairs of coloured glass buttons joined together by a short, linked chain.

By 1715, this gave way to pairs of decoratively painted or jewelled studs, often diamonds connected with an ornate gold link – thus the cufflink was born.

With the onset of the Industrial Revolution (c. 1760–1850), mass production methods enabled the manufacture of low cost cufflinks, which led to greater variety; and businessmen from varying classes began wearing cufflinks and stud sets. Single or double-length (French) cufflink designs and shapes are now widely available.

14. Violet Darkling's 18ct rose gold plate cufflinks with amethyst eyes are a sleek adaptation of the fossa, a Madagascan predator. They 'bite' the shirt cuff with their teeth in a novel take on the traditional cufflink.

15. Katie Hillier

16. 'Bunny Love' ring, glowing heart ring, and bubble heart ring, designed by Katie Hillier.

Katie Hillier is a designer whose skills traverse jewellery, accessory and handbag design. She has worked for many influential luxury houses including Marc by Marc Jacobs, Hugo Boss, Luella, Clements Ribeiro, Bill Amberg, Giles Deacon, Salvatore Ferragamo and Stella McCartney. She is also creative director of her own luxury brand, Hillier.

What formal training and background do you have?

I studied for a degree in fashion at the University of Westminster (UK). I did a work placement at *Dazed and Confused* where I assisted Katie Grand, and after that I worked as a photographer's assistant for John Akehurst. Eventually I started work with Luella Bartley (fashion designer) as her assistant.

How do you identify the zeitgeist or upcoming trends in the fickle world of fashion?

You have to do what you think feels right and relevant for the moment.

How would you define your own brand and what was the impetus for its launch?

Hillier is about me and my friends, about the girls I know and work with, places I have travelled to and things I have collected. It's a very personal project. I have had a lot of satisfaction working for the people who I have worked with, but I wanted to do something personal and fun.

What is your design ethos?

Luxury with a wink.

What do you think constitutes good design?

Something that you want to live with forever.

Which three pieces of advice you would give those just entering the industry?

Be confident about your opinion, make it relevant, try to gain a very broad set of skills within the industry; it will help you to understand why you are designing the product. Try to have an understanding of business; it's not all about pretty things, you have to make sure it sells!

Jewellery Styles

Lara Bohinc

17
18

17. Lara Bohinc

18. 'Collision' bracelet from the Solaris collection made with cubic zirconia and black onyx, designed by Lara Bohinc.

Today, issue W

Lara Bohinc's luxury goods company is renowned for its design, craftsmanship and quality. Design references span the classical and contemporary with a modern and bold use of precious metals and discreet but identifiable designs.

What made you choose jewellery design as a career?

I studied graphics and industrial design and that left quite a big mark on my work. I design everything on computer and, as a product designer, I consider production techniques and how things are made. I realized jewellery is really a combination of fashion, architecture, and graphic design, these are all areas in which I am interested.

You are now an international brand. When you first started out was it hard establishing yourself?

You always start by yourself – I did everything, I designed the jewellery, I made the jewellery, I did the cleaning, the accounts, I sold the jewellery – and then slowly as the business grows you start outsourcing to other people. Now I'm finally at that stage where I'm just concerned with the design.

Who or what most inspires you stylistically, and which people do you particularly admire in design?

I like lots of artefacts, both past and present. I like Zaha Hadid, sculptors such as Naum Gabo. For jewellery I like Sophia Vari and Raymond Templier. These are people who are iconic within periods of design. They are people who stand as the beacons of the quality that you try to achieve with your own work.

What are the key ways in which you market/distribute the brand globally?

We do appointments at our own showroom. We have a press office that loans samples internationally and issues press releases twice a year to journalists, freelancers and buyers.

You have expanded into bags and accessories; what was the impetus for this portfolio expansion?

The aim was always to build a small, new luxury house. All the luxury houses have this synergy between accessories – mainly leather goods, scarves and jewellery – so that was always the aim, to complete the offer.

...ociety is much more conscious of ...s of sustainability than it was in the past. ...recognize to a greater degree that we are ...art of one interdependent global community. **Increasingly, consumers want the jewellery that they are buying to meet certain ethical standards, for example, that its raw materials do not fund wars; that their extraction does not harm the environment or use toxic chemicals and that indigenous people, children and workforces have not been exploited during its making.**

People care about where their purchases have come from; they want to know what impact they have had on the environment. As a result, some designers are responding by using responsibly produced metals. The use of fair trade precious metals allow for designs that are better aligned to jewellery's emotional and symbolic value, restoring the idea that the way in which a jewellery design is created is essential to its overall value.

19. 'Discreetly bizarre' ring made with Fairtrade Fairmined gold and trillion cut fire-citrine, designed by Linnie Mclarty.

20. The jewellery designer Pippa Small is renowned for her work with indigenous tribes and communities.

19

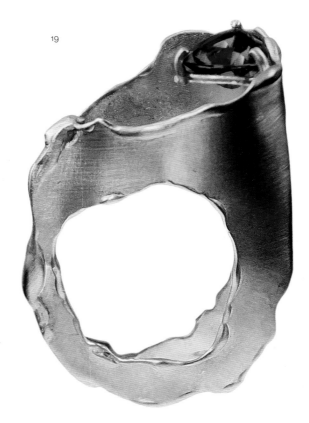

Conflict or blood diamonds

'Conflict' or 'blood' diamonds are diamonds mined in parts of Africa, which are illegally exploited to fund rebel militias in a series of wars in which many people die. Countries associated with conflict diamonds include Angola, Sierra Leone, the Democratic Republic of Congo, Liberia and Guinea.

Dirty gold

Gold that is mined where there is little or no consideration given to environmental and/or social aspects of production is called 'dirty gold'.

'The basis of so much in life is human relationships – there is a universal appeal in adornment, for so many diverse reasons and meanings – it is so exciting that the making of jewellery can lead to empowering communities and individuals so they have both creative expression and control over their lives through the generating of collections and revenue.'
Pippa Small

'Raw Crown' ring made with
18ct Fairtrade Fairmined gold and
9ct rough diamonds, designed by
Hattie Rickards.

21

The Kimberley Process

The Kimberley Process is an intergovernmental organization implemented as a direct result of concerns regarding illicit diamonds entering the legitimate diamond trade and funding rebel movements. It strives to certify diamonds as 'conflict free' and is enforced in all EU countries and in around 40 other countries worldwide. It works to regulate the flow of rough diamonds and to exclude conflict diamonds from the supply chain.

The Kimberley Process is supported by a code of conduct introduced by the World Diamond Council. Launched in 2003, the Kimberley Process Certification Scheme (KPCS) requires diamond traders to present certificates of origin, to warrant that the diamonds have come from legitimate sources not involved in funding conflict and in compliance with United Nations resolutions.

However, controversy has arisen around the Kimberley Process. In 2011, the NGO Global Witness, one of the main participants, withdrew its support from the Kimberley Process, saying that 'over the past nine years, KP had failed to evolve or address the clear links between diamonds, violence and tyranny.' (The *Guardian*, 5 December 2011)

Jewellery Styles

Fairtrade and Fairmined certified gold

Fairtrade and Fairmined certified gold is the world's first independent ethical certification system for gold. It guarantees that the gold has been responsibly mined from small-scale mines in South America. Many of these miners are subsistence miners (also called artisanal) consisting of women and children using hand tools.

Fairtrade and Fairmined gold certification is the result of a joint partnership between Fairtrade Labelling Organizations International (FLO) and the Alliance for Responsible Mining (ARM). Global initiatives such as ARM and Corporación Oro Verde have been established with the aim of enhancing equity and wellbeing in artisan and small-scale miners. They are tasked with improving social, environmental and labour practices, establishing good governance and implementing ecosystem restoration practices while providing a fair, regular source of income to miners, their families and their communities.

Such initiatives are driven to set standards for responsible mining, making the process an economically sound, socially and environmentally responsible activity. New international Fairtrade standards and a Fairtrade mark have boosted the standards of the ethical gold market allowing designers and consumers to source, produce and buy responsibly.

Organizations such as 'Made' Africa and the Turquoise Mountain Foundation in Kabul in Afghanistan bring together indigenous communities with designers from the West. The aim is to provide an exchange of ideas and training for local artisans who are encouraged to earn a living from their work and heritage, which can drastically improve lives and rejuvenate communities.

22. 'Discreetly bizarre' ring made with Fairtrade Fairmined gold and 22ct rough cut ruby, designed by Linnie Mclarty.

22

Interview: Lara Bohinc > **Ethical practice** > Case study: Ethical design

Pippa Small is a jewellery designer actively working with indigenous communities. Pippa studied anthropology and then completed an MA in medical anthropology. She started making jewellery to fund her degree and soon collaborated with fashion houses Gucci, Nicole Farhi, and Chloé. Later, her two interests merged while working on craft initiatives with indigenous communities helping them to research their traditional designs to generate self-sufficiency and income. She divides her time between her anthropological work and jewellery collections.

23

23. Kuna women are heavily adorned in gold and beaded jewellery, gold nose rings and beautiful charms of gold butterflies, birds and sea creatures. They rouge their cheeks and paint a fine black line down the length of their nose.

24. Pippa Small's Kuna gold butterfly necklace was inspired by the Kuna people.

One such project centred on the design of a collection with the Kuna Indians of Panama in Central America, a remarkably independent, culturally intact tribe and craftspeople with a territory on the Caribbean coast, with whom Pippa worked to create her collection. The Kuna believe that gold is purifying and sacred, that it is the 'veins of Mother Earth'. They do not believe in mining and have refused large-scale mining concessions on their land. They pan the gold from the rivers and make flat sheets of the gold, which are then hammered, cut, and etched.

'I was inspired by the women's designs from their molas (traditional geometric designs on fabric). We worked on cascading waterfalls of tumbling gold butterflies, chains of disks with the mola patterns carefully engraved on each and on earrings that glitter and flash in the sun. This was a new idea to bring the women's designs into the sphere of the male gold workers. On the last day when the women in the village tried on the finished pieces and gave their approval with excitement about this novel direction, I was excited.'

24

25

26

25. Stephen Webster

26. 'Classic Crystal Haze' ring made with turquoise, quartz and white diamonds, designed by Stephen Webster.

Stephen Webster is founder and creative director of Stephen Webster and creative director of Garrard.

What is your formal training/ background?

I trained at the Medway College in Kent, UK, then I took an apprenticeship in Canada when I finished my course and was very lucky to work with a man with an incredible passion and knowledge of gems. The different stones I was given fascinated me and I was allowed complete freedom to work with them. This was the job where I built my confidence as a designer and maker and learned how to communicate with a client.

Why did you choose jewellery?

I was originally planning on studying fashion design but by chance walked into a jewellery design class rather than the fashion design room. The flames, noise, chemicals and shiny objects were instantly appealing and much more up my alley than fashion design. I guess it was a good choice as 36 years later I am still at it!

How important is ethical practice to you? Can you tell us more about your involvement in raising awareness of this in relation to diamond and gold mining and why you are passionate about the subject?

Earlier in the year I visited gold mines in Peru accompanied by Fairtrade in order to see first-hand the difference between Fairmined gold and a regular gold supply chain. I have since become a spokesman for Fairtrade gold and our partnership with Forevermark now allows us to be certain that our diamonds are responsibly sourced and cared for at every stage of their journey, as well as being among the finest in the world. More and more consumers are questioning the origins of the things they buy and Stephen Webster likes to ask the same questions.

27

28

27–28. Examples of Stephen Webster's couture designs.

What is your design ethos?

It has always been my passion to cultivate jewellery collections that push all creative boundaries; are high on innovation and are unreservedly cool. All of my work is a reflection of my personality. I am fortunate that selfishly, I have pursued topics and inspirations from my life's experiences and translated them into our many collections. Within all of them there is vibrancy. I am a cheery fellow.

What are your biggest passions?

Coloured gemstones have always been one of my passions. Twenty years ago I started to experiment with layering precious gemstones with a layer of clear quartz, creating an incredible effect that has become the very core of our business today.

My love of music has really influenced my style; it has been my passion from very early days. I have always striven to bring something new to the jewellery table. It is important to me that all my pieces are a combination of fine-quality materials, fine craftsmanship, considered design and that bit of an edge.

Who do you admire in design and what inspires you creatively?

I've always loved 'Dragonfly Woman' by René Lalique. Something about the combination of fantasy, myth, use of materials, craftsmanship and sheer brilliance make this my favourite piece.

I've always taken inspiration from so many great jewellery designers and traditions; I try to take traditional themes and create a modern twist to them. However I'd say that mostly my inspiration comes from the objects, sights and people around me: the sea, gems, film noir, tattoos, architecture, broken glass, even fish bones.

29. 'Forget me Knot' cascade earrings made with white gold and blue sapphires, designed by Stephen Webster.

30. 'Forget me Knot' crystal haze drop earrings made with white gold, green agate and black and white diamonds, designed by Stephen Webster.

You are also creative director of fine jewellery house Garrard. How do you balance Garrard heritage with your own unique signature?

Garrard style has always been difficult to define due to the diversity of the products on offer. In the recent past there has been a shift to produce collections that retain elements of the classic DNA of the brand while providing a product for today's consumer. Perfect examples of this are 'Wings' and the new 'Star and Garter' collections. Our new collections remain true to this philosophy while striving to keep the product creative and exciting.

How does a collection evolve?

As a brand, Garrard has such an amazing history that the best place to start with a new collection is in the archives. It really is a destination that offers an extraordinary selection of treasures, covering all the related trades and crafts surrounding the jewellery and silversmithing industries.

How many collections do you work on in a year?

Generally one fine jewellery collection, but there are always special projects and guest designers.

What are the challenges/highlights of directing a brand with such heritage?

I relish that I am the creative director of a brand whose archives tell the story of the glory days of being the Crown Jeweller. Two hundred and seventy-five years brings some great anecdotes, characters and products. From Robert Garrard's rococo-style table pieces to the many gifts made by Garrard and designed by Prince Albert for his wife Queen Victoria. The archive under my office is like a private wing of the V&A. From the Duke of Wellington, who would arrive on his white charger, to Barry Gibb who was partial to the odd gold chain from Garrard, this is a story like no other.

31. Couture cascade drop earrings made with 18ct white gold set with pavé white diamonds and pear-shaped zultanite stones, designed by Stephen Webster.

32. Couture cocktail ring made with 18ct white gold set with pavé white diamonds and zultanite, designed by Stephen Webster.

Over the next few years I hope I can produce collections that connect with a modern consumer, while respectfully giving a nod to the heritage and respect that being the Crown Jeweller for over 150 years can command.

What in your opinion makes a good design?

Jewellery has to be more and more individual and extraordinary. The new buyers of luxury want to surround themselves with things that say something about themselves, their lives and the choices they make.

What three pieces of advice would you give to a young designer?

The first piece of advice would be to never underestimate the value of advice you may get from people with experience in your field.

Provide an original idea. This doesn't happen too often but it will be the thing that people can never take away from you and will give you credibility from then on. Compare it to the breakthrough album.

Stick to what you believe in. No matter what others may think of me I tried to change the rules, I have stuck with it and now it's my normality.

What makes a good junior designer, what do you look for?

Patience and good training from an expert; this may seem a little traditionalist but this is a slow traditional business with very few overnight stars. However, if you make it, it is also one of the greatest industries. We work with the finest materials, create things that make people happy and if you are lucky, get to see the world too.

Case study: Ethical design > Interview: Stephen Webster > Project: The customer

Consider who your potential customers are and begin by creating a profile for them. As a designer, it is really helpful to identify your customers so that you can build designs that are appropriate for their lifestyle. A successful designer will consider the market in which their customers consume and the price points relevant to their chosen market.

33

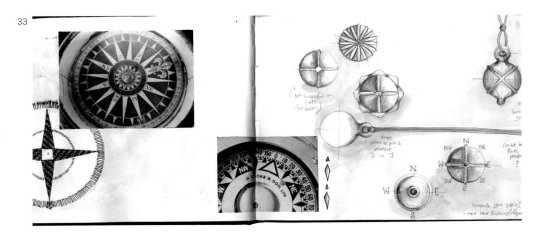

34

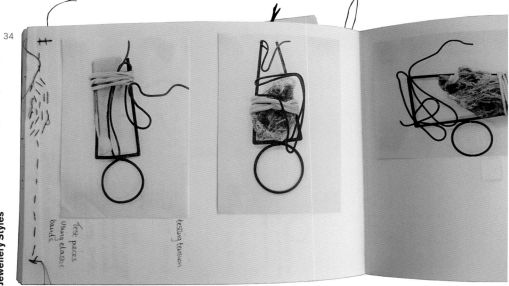

33. Student sketchbook by Elizabeth Campbell, ECA, Edinburgh University, UK.

34. Student sketchbook by Mari Ebbitt ECA, Edinburgh University, UK.

35. Student work by Rebecca Vigers ECA, Edinburgh University, UK.

35

- First of all, think about where your potential customers live and what their lifestyles are like and ask the following questions.

- How will your designs connect with customers?

- What stores do your customers frequent and which brands do they gravitate towards?

- What do they do for a living?

- How do they enjoy their leisure time?

- What do they spend their disposable income on?

- Do a competitor shop (comp shopping) where you identify and analyse your perceived competitors. It is important to find a niche that you can exploit. In this way you can start to build a story and a USP (unique selling proposition).

- A valuable exercise is to visit the stockists you envisage selling your jewellery collections to and look at their customer demographic and the brands and designers that they stock. How will your products compare?

- Look at the market and identify how brands interact with customers through marketing and visual merchandising.

- Look at the price points, presentation and craftsmanship – what do they tell you about the customers?

'Rotarex' showpiece necklace,
Akris cuffs and Akris earrings
made with Swarovski Elements,
designed by Manik Mercian.

...mmercial jewellery collection ...ee of research, attention to ... of materials and price, and ...ng of the customer and the market. Designers absorb ideas and references from a variety of cultural sources, such as history, film, music, literature, and art. In this chapter we explore the sources of inspiration and the importance of research.

1. Tahitian pearl brooch designed by Shaun Leane for the actress Sarah Jessica Parker.

2. Original design sketch for Shaun Leane's Tahitian pearl brooch.

1

Designers working for a jewellery house will follow the style of the brand's 'DNA'; this reflects the visual identity for which the brand is well known. It is compiled from a variety of sources, including the company's historical archives, customer analysis, famous products, emotive phrases that typify the brand, logos and colour palettes. Designers at fine jewellery houses combine iconic statements from the company's historical archives with the designers' interpretations to create contemporary designs imbued with both a sense of heritage and modernity, making them relevant to today's consumer.

Sources of inspiration can be varied and diverse: visiting museums, galleries, trade fairs, antique markets, travelling and experiencing other cultures can all influence a designer's creative universe.

Research should be collated to form a visual library of information, which will help you to derive your own unique design signature over time. Designers should be familiar with other design disciplines, so that they can place their work in a cultural context, provoking fresh ideas on the use of materials, processes and proportions.

Modes of research

There are three forms of research in jewellery design: primary, secondary and tertiary.

Primary research is unique to the designer and is made up of personal photography, drawings and thoughts.

Secondary research is material that already exists, which has been created by someone else; this includes art, printed and digital material, books, journals and reports.

Tertiary research comprises magazines, newspapers and Internet sources such as Wikipedia, which has been condensed from 'common knowledge' on the topic and is intended for a broad public audience. (Remember to check your facts from an authoritative source not just from Wikipedia.)

It is important for designers to find a common theme or distinctive 'handwriting' that runs through their designs, this helps to carve a niche and ensures work endures over time. Designers may develop specific shapes within their collections, which can easily be identified at a glance as their style. Acclaimed fine jewellery house Shaun Leane is recognizable for its use of thorns, horns and tusks, which Shaun Leane first created for the late fashion designer Alexander McQueen.

2

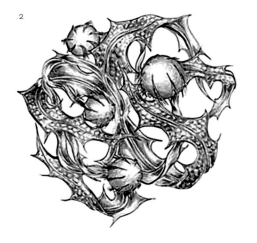

Sources of inspiration > Trend forecasting

Jewellery and watch trade fairs

Being aware of the market means assessing competitor advertising campaigns and visual merchandising, studying trend reports and journals, looking at street style and current products.

Jewellery designers regularly visit trade fairs. This is where brands showcase their new collections and manufacturers display their products. Here, you can gather trend-forecasting information from the vast array of exhibitors, order samples and view the latest products and components such as stones, chains and findings (fastenings). It is an opportunity for designers to discover the latest trends and meet with clients to discuss new additions to their catalogues.

Designers can also source manufacturers and materials. Many manufacturers have minimum orders and for samples and small orders they may levy a surcharge or shipping costs. They will always request a business card from visitors and trade buyers wishing to place a sample order.

3

4

3. ModAmont Fair, part of Première Vision, Paris is a key destination for fashion jewellery brands.

4. BASELWORLD is Europe's largest and most prestigious watch and jewellery fair.

Trade fairs

BASELWORLD Watch and Jewellery Fair (Switzerland)

Hong Kong Jewellery Fair (China)

Inhorgenta, Munich (Germany)

International Jewellery London (IJL), (UK)

JCK, Las Vegas (USA)

ModAmont, Paris (France)

New York Gift Fair (USA)

Première Classe, Paris (France)

Sieraad International Jewellery Art Fair, Amsterdam (Holland)

Spring Fair, Birmingham (UK)

Vicenza Fair (Italy)

5

Designers have to create innovative and unique creations, so it is imperative that they stay abreast of prevailing trends. Trend forecasting companies provide designers with a wide range of research across the spectrum of design and retail. They take into account key indicators for technology, consumer trends, retail developments and global and economic forecasts. Futurologists will create bespoke trend packages and analyses that are tailored to a specific brand's needs.

Trend forecasting services identify cultural trends, colour palettes, new technologies and styles for the seasons ahead. These are presented in trend forecasting books, are accessible online on a subscription basis, and designers can attend twice yearly seminars. Trend forecasts are intended to be interpreted by a designer, without slavishly following them.

Social media is also an inexhaustible pool of information that reflects the collective consciousness and emerging trends. Community platforms such as Stylehive, Tumblr, Twitter, Facebook, YouTube, Kaboodle, Polyvore and StumbleUpon are free sources of information.
The information on fashion and jewellery blogs may also have good pointers to what is destined to be an upcoming trend.

Trend forecasters

www.thefuturelaboratory.com

www.tjfgroup.com

www.trendstop.com

www.wgsn.com

Essential Research

5. Trend research spans many aspects of design including colour palettes, economic and cultural developments, historical and contemporary themes.

Using trend research

Lauren Egan-Fowler is a freelance accessories designer. She tracks and researches trends as part of the design process.

For Lauren Egan-Fowler, trend research is a constant process influenced by her surroundings – from television to graphic advertising styles, music, exhibitions, and comp shopping (UK and international, new and vintage). She also visits trade shows, bars, clubs and restaurants, and travels to festivals and markets.

When she collects images to create trend boards, many come from Internet blog sites such as Style Bubble and PurseBlog, magazines, trend prediction companies such as WGSN and PeclersParis and also websites such as Vogue.com, Elle.com and Style.com.

Historical research is also vital; researched trends are both a starting point to focus attention and give direction. There are also lots of classic and successful formulae that work time and again once they are given a new twist. Knowing about these before starting a project can be useful.

The trends and the research give a great overview of everything that is happening and allows you to see how your ideas can bring something fresh, new and exciting, and possibly fill gaps in the market.

As part of her work, Lauren might take a jewellery collection and develop it into an accessory line, such as bags. In order to do this, she studies the research that has gone into the jewellery collection. She looks at shapes, patterns, metal colours, branding, styling features and logos that could then be translated into the leather goods. Jewellery shape, detail, and colour can translate easily and literally into hardware that can be used on leather goods, for example, metal locks, plates, zip pullers, and chain straps.

Patterns, shapes and decorative detailing from the jewellery can be translated into leather and fabric through jacquard, embossing, perforations and studded decoration.

The colour palette that Lauren uses is very important. She starts by researching seasonal colour trends. However, she feels that a large amount of colour choices are based on personal preferences, research and ultimately gut feeling.

Lauren studies the potential saleability of her designs based on sales information and performance of similar products. She also considers where the product is being manufactured and the client brief or target market, and looks at trends for this area.

Materials are sourced from suppliers and in particular at trade shows, such as Lineapelle and Première Vision, which are very important for sourcing new materials, ideas and trends. Material sourcing is dictated by price and quality, as well as the brief and target market. It is important to follow developments in this area and see what competitors are doing.

Essential Research

6

6. Lauren Egan-Fowler's 'A good vintage' moodboard.

When starting to develop and create a design you will be using all kinds of sources and materials to inspire you. It is important to keep your research material accessible. You may want to refer to it over time and building up your own library of visual resources will help you in the future.

7. Archived objects and jewellery collected from flea markets and suppliers can be a fruitful source of inspiration.

Archiving

Designers and companies keep archives of the reference material that they have found useful in helping them to create their designs. This may include archiving a library of product catalogues and samples, and materials such as stones, findings and chain. A brand archive also includes discontinued products and discarded prototypes. The latter are often revisited and reworked or used as influences for future collections.

Collections that have been a commercial success are often evolved and extended the following season with 'line extensions' (new designs). They may constitute versions of a 'hero' product in a new metal, or set with different stones and the archive is a useful tool during this process. Hero products are a company's best-selling items.

Magazines and books

Designers gain a great deal of inspiration from fashion and lifestyle magazines and books, which offer a global view of fashion, jewellery and accessories.

Some libraries have archives of magazines such as *Harper's Bazaar*, *Vogue* and *Elle* and many magazine titles are available online. There are specialist bookshops and newsagents that carry independent and international titles. Street-style images can be found in dedicated magazines, and on blogs and websites. Looking at all kinds of sources, including international ones, can help to broaden your knowledge of different styles and how individuals around the world approach jewellery and adornment.

Sources for fashion magazines and books

www.assouline.com

www.avabooks.com

www.foyles.co.uk

www.magculture.com

www.magmabooks.com

www.taschen.com

www.thamesandhudson.com

Many small jewellery brands lack the infrastructure to gather and analyse accurate market and marketing information. Bigger brands are able to define every aspect of their customer through sales, specialist marketing information and dedicated business development departments.

However, a developed intuition and an overall awareness of the market and fashion and jewellery trends will help a young designer to become a commercial success. It is important to analyse competitors carefully, and many designers will identify and focus on a particular niche or product (such as unusual engagement rings) as a focused way of entering the market. This can then be expanded based on best-selling hero products.

Important considerations include whether a design is intended for everyday wear or a special occasion, which similar products are available and what price the market will bear; all of which will influence the cost, weight and scale of your designs.

8

Moodboards

Moodboards are used as a tool to effectively communicate ideas. They are an amalgamation of visual references sourced from personal research and set the scene for a designer's collection. Grouping key trends, images, colours, words or themes, moodboards convey your research in an organized manner and act as a consistent reference during the design process.

It is important to expand on your visual research on a weekly basis and try to push yourself beyond your immediate interests. In the digital age, designers can source an endless number of images to feed their personal narrative, and photography is often a useful means of capturing visual information on the move.

As a designer, you should start sketching once you have refined your ideas and have enough material from which to choose a direction.

8. Scrapbooks incorporating collages, poems, words and personal research.

9. Dorothée Pugnet's 'Personal Universe' moodboard documenting nostalgic and vintage themes.

Collecting

Collecting objects or materials is also a useful process to accompany moodboard presentations. Many designers have a penchant for creating jewellery from 'bricolage' (found objects), manipulating or subverting everyday, mundane objects to create whimsical jewellery. For example, fabrics and graphic prints have the potential to become an etched pattern; a matchstick or a piece of coral can be cast into metal and set with semi-precious stones. Style icons past and present as well as film, art, literature and music also have the power to inspire a collection.

10. Artist, prop-maker and jewellery designer Jessica de Lotz creates whimsical pieces from found objects and vintage items.

11. 'Peeping Tom' winking eye ring made from a vintage doll's eye within a *fleur-de-lis* claw by Jessica de Lotz.

12

12. Alice Menter's handwoven 'Joni' necklace made with gold-plated hexagonal nuts and lengths of red suede.

13. As a contemporary *bricoleur* Claire English produces modern heirlooms incorporating gathered themes and stories.

Style icons

Iris Apfel, Isabella Blow, Louise Brooks, Coco Chanel, Salvador Dali, Daphne Guinness, Amanda Harlech, Audrey Hepburn, Grace Jones, Jackie Kennedy, Lady Gaga, Grace Kelly, Eva Peron, Anna Piaggi, Carine Roitfield, Elsa Schiaparelli, Elizabeth Taylor, and Diana Vreeland.

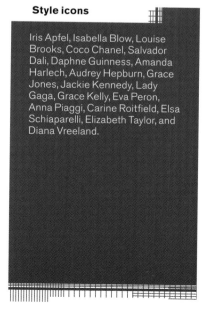

13

Shaun Leane

14. Shaun Leane

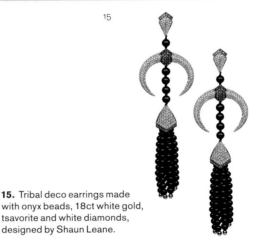

15. Tribal deco earrings made with onyx beads, 18ct white gold, tsavorite and white diamonds, designed by Shaun Leane.

Shaun Leane is founder and CEO of the fine jewellery house Shaun Leane.

What is your background?

I left school at 15 and enrolled on a one-year jewellery design and making course at Kingsway College, UK. I fell in love with jewellery, and at 16 went on to do an apprenticeship for a company called English Traditional Jewellery in Hatton Garden in London, UK.

I was taught by two goldsmithing masters for 13 years; seven years as an apprentice making some of the most beautiful fine jewellery, learning every element, which included working on diamond solitaires and tiaras, as well as antique restoration for some of Bond Street's (London) fine jewellery houses.

In a moment of serendipity, I met Alexander McQueen. We had similar backgrounds and a great respect for attention to detail. He had trained at Savile Row and I was trained in Hatton Garden.

We were the same age and he was studying fashion at Central Saint Martins in London. I was really inspired by his work, as he was with mine, so he suggested that I create work for his catwalk shows. I was a bit daunted at first, being classically conditioned to work in precious metals and stones and having never worked in silver nor with non-precious metals.

Alexander suggested that if I could create beautiful miniature sculptures in fine materials, I should just think bigger and out of the box. I began to teach myself silversmithing, to meet the demand for what we would begin to create for the catwalk.

It was a great platform, taking my classical skills and applying a modern approach to creating powerful, iconic pieces, which have been exhibited in museums around the world. The pieces raised questions about the notions and boundaries of jewellery, while being beautifully made using traditional jewellery techniques.

Essential Research

16

17

16. Black leather cuff made with
18ct white gold and diamond sabre
tusk, designed by Shaun Leane.

17. Interlocking ring set made with 18ct
white gold and diamonds, designed by
Shaun Leane.

How did you collaborate with McQueen?

Our vision was very similar, I would look at the moodboards, sketches and silhouettes for the collection and we'd bounce ideas off each other; creating jewellery that fitted the concept. For example, the coil corset that I made for McQueen (see page 013), evolved from the necklace I'd created for the singer Björk, McQueen asked me to create one for the body; which really pushed the boundaries for me in design as well as technically as a fine jeweller. This was when my work moved towards sculpture.

How did you start out?

In 1998, Harvey Nichols approached me, having seen my work for McQueen, and wanting to buy my first collection; at the time I didn't have one. I took elements of the signature shapes I'd created for McQueen such as the tusk, the crown of thorns and the horn, and created my first signature silver collections, fusing fine craftsmanship with cutting-edge design.

Fine jewellery collections then evolved and the atelier now has many facets, including bespoke work for private clients, jewellery collaborations and fine jewellery. My ultimate goal as a young apprentice was to create museum-worthy pieces.

We've worked with numerous collaborators including Givenchy, Boucheron, the Shiseido Group and Daphne Guinness, each with our house's signature handwriting. We work on two collections a year, one fine and two silver (one for men and one for women).

Our atelier designs and makes the pieces; while I'm a classically trained goldsmith we are inspired by the modern. We have both classically trained craftsmen and a CAD designer, which is a good balance between using traditional jewellery techniques and new technology. We draw every fine technical detail and I oversee the making of everything to ensure that the handwriting is consistent.

Shaun Leane

How has your house evolved?

You could say I was the Jekyll and Hyde of the jewellery industry; by day I was making classics for English traditional jewellery and by night creating skeleton corsets and crown of thorns for McQueen, with no design constraints. This is where I began to use my traditional jewellery skills to create pieces which are innovative in both design and materials. I'm flattered and honoured that these pieces have gone on to inspire other jewellers over the years.

What is your ethos?

My ethos is that jewellery should be just as beautiful from the back as it is from the front. Our atelier's designs are refined, elegant but confident.

What is good design?

Designing a piece that makes the wearer feel confident and beautiful utilizing materials and craftsmanship and fusing these together to create a stunning *objet d'art* to wear.

What advice would you give to a young designer?

Learn craftsmanship and understand the creation of a piece, which helps with the design. Never be scared to push the boundaries and follow your vision, and think out of the box. Out of the wildest ideas, you can find a beautiful element.

18

18. The original design drawing for *Contra Mundum* ('against the world') a bespoke diamond glove designed by Shaun Leane and Daphne Guinness.

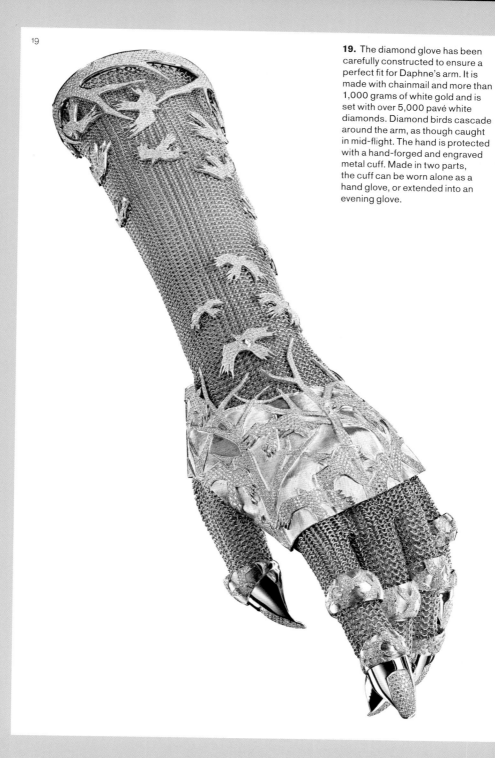

19

19. The diamond glove has been carefully constructed to ensure a perfect fit for Daphne's arm. It is made with chainmail and more than 1,000 grams of white gold and is set with over 5,000 pavé white diamonds. Diamond birds cascade around the arm, as though caught in mid-flight. The hand is protected with a hand-forged and engraved metal cuff. Made in two parts, the cuff can be worn alone as a hand glove, or extended into an evening glove.

In order to create a moodboard you can gather sources of inspiration from many different sources. Visit markets and trade shows, galleries and museums, make notes in your sketchbook and photograph interesting examples of design. Walk around key shopping districts and absorb window installations and study jewellery presentations so that you are connected to the commercial and artistic environment that is going on all around you. Eventually this will become second nature and will expand your visual vocabulary, which will form an ongoing and valuable part of your creative journey.

20. Personal work by BA student Ciara Bowles, of ECA, Edinburgh University, UK, showing the development of initial sketches, colour references and texture examples, which could become part of a moodboard.

Imagine that you have a customer and need to create a design; in order to do this you need to build a moodboard, or a series of moodboards. First, you need to consider who your customer is, for example:

- What type of lifestyle does your customer lead?

- How does your customer spend his or her leisure time?

- What does your customer wear?

- Where does your customer shop?

- Which brands is your customer likely to be interested in?

You can use the information collected during your research for the project on pages 058–9.

Compile your research into specific groups, such as historical and cultural, colour and texture, materials and images. Create a series of mood or inspiration boards that convey your design ideas.

You may find it helpful to write yourself a short brief or story summing up your inspiration, which may include quotes from poetry or literature or a key set of phrases; or focus on a particular genre or character from history or film – this will sit alongside your moodboard and explain your thinking.

It is important to stimulate your mind and expose yourself to new ideas beyond your immediate areas of interest, it will keep you creatively energized, challenged and inspired!

21. Finished pieces by BA student Ciara Bowles, ECA, Edinburgh University, UK.

21

Interview: Shaun Leane > **Project: Creating a moodboard**

'Nightshade' cocktail ring made
with 18ct white gold with pavé
set diamonds and amethysts
and 18ct yellow gold stamen,
designed by Mackinnon.

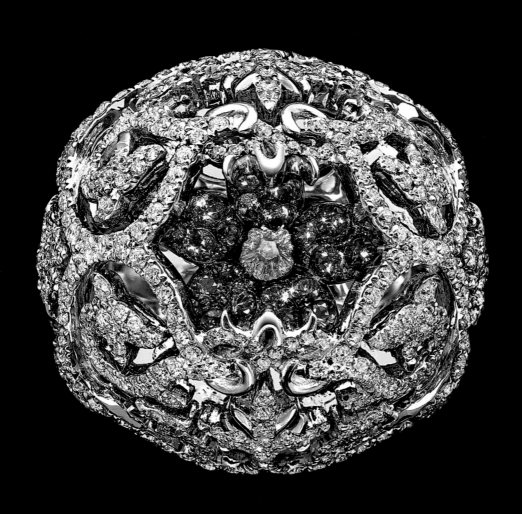

Studying jewellery design allows you to develop your creativity, expand your professional studies and respond to a series of technical projects and contextual studies. This chapter is intended to guide you in the development of your own designs.

It is important to have a comprehensive understanding of how a piece is made. While in Europe designers no longer have to serve a traditional seven-year apprenticeship, it is still imperative to learn and understand the fundamental skills and craftsmanship required to make and manufacture a piece of jewellery.

This chapter explores how a brief is approached. It also looks at the use of CAD (computer-aided design) and CAM (computer-aided manufacturing. A brief is a statement of intent, proposal or outline of your concept; it can take the form of a short description and should be evocative of your idea. Jewellery has to exist within a context, drawn from history, culture and contemporary ideas and as a designer you create your own context for your collection. You may find it useful to write a narrative for your approach that takes its inspiration from fantasy, everyday life, film or literature, and which could form the basis of your research.

1

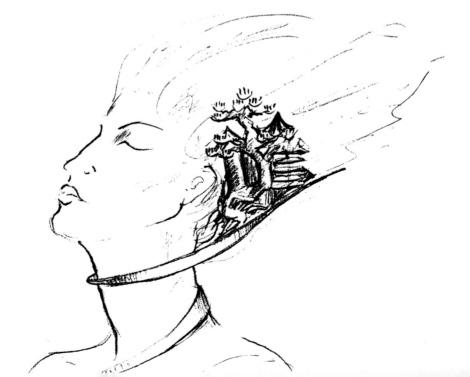

2

Outstanding designers are fastidious about the depth of their research and references. The greater the preparation that is put into this early design stage, the easier it is to make decisions during the sampling and manufacturing phases.

The jewellery house Erickson Beamon (see interview on page 160) created a headpiece for the catwalk fashion show for Givenchy in 2000. Here you can see some of the early design stages and the finished piece.

3

1–2. Drawing and sketch for the Givenchy winged headpiece by Erickson Beamon.

3. The final headpiece shown at the catwalk show for the fashion house Givenchy.

The designer's brief > Designing from your research

Designers use their research to develop their concepts. During this stage, designers bring together the key aspects of their research and draw on these influences to create the final design drawings. They use their research as a visual resource to explore permutations and ideas.

It is important for designers to remain flexible and open to change during this phase as, over time, the prices and availability of precious metals, materials and stones may vary, which might affect their design brief and costs.

4

Option 1

Sketchbooks

Sketchbooks record designers' creative journeys and thought processes and they are continually evolving. They are made up of collages of images, pencil drawings, materials, words, and found media. Sketchbooks provide a format to explore creative ideas freely and are a fundamental part of the design process. Collages enable designers to think through details and preferences before working on fully rendered illustrations.

It is important to remain flexible at this stage of the design development and to explore lots of permutations before realizing your final ideas. Your sketchbook should illustrate the breadth and detail of your thinking and analysis in a dynamic and invigorating way.

Option 2

Option 3

Design Creation

4. A sketch of the 'Lianhua' earrings designed by Sarah Ho.

5. The fully realized couture 'Lianhua' earrings designed by Sarah Ho.

5

Design drawings

Design drawings are fundamental to the visual communication of a collection. Designers generally use a combination of hand sketches and drawings created using various software packages to present finished designs, which are accompanied by range plans, technical drawings and specification documents.

Design drawings created in the traditional fine jewellery style use watercolours, gouache (renderings) or pen and ink, which require a flair for drawing. The development of software packages has enabled students to replicate industry standard processes and techniques when presenting their portfolios. It is a worthwhile investment in today's fast-paced design environment to master some computer skills that will enable you to use these software packages.

If you lack outstanding drawing skills, or feel out of your depth with CAD, it is still possible to realize your ideas and designs in a variety of ways. Some designers will evolve a design by using a mixture of simple pencil sketches combined with 3D materials and model-making techniques that utilize materials such as wax, clay, beads, chain and wire. You can then use professional services to create a CAD file for you, based on the model.

6–7. Drawing and final piece for the 'Aurora' necklace by Sarah Ho for Sarah Ho Couture.

6

7

8

8. Design drawing of Lalique's 'Vesta' necklace, Goddess of Fire.

9. 'Ghandi' earrings finished paint up, designed by Ana de Costa.

10. Ana de Costa's 'Ghandi' 20ct emerald earrings with cognac diamonds. These ethical earrings were created in collaboration with mining company, Gemfields.

9

10

Technical drawings

Finished designs are accompanied by technical sketches (specs or mechanical drawings), which give the dimensions of the piece. They outline the side, front and top view of the design, as well as the measurements and the materials the piece will be made in. Specs are closely followed by the product developer, model maker (or prototype maker) and the manufacturer, who initially realizes the design drawing in the form of a wax or metal prototype. This allows the designer to see a three-dimensional (3D) object, which can then be revised to ensure that the size and weight is correct before manufacturing the finished product.

11. Hand-painted design drawing of 'Chrysanthemum' pendant by Daisuke Sakaguchi.

12. Lalique 'Vibrante' pendant made with 9ct yellow gold, amber crystal, champagne diamonds and pompom on a black cord.

12

11

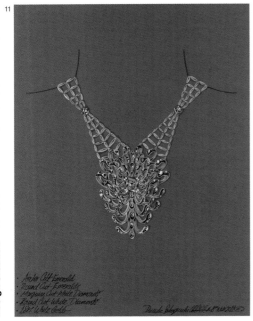

Design Creation

13

4.8mm

9mm

Ø 42mm

Ø 40mm

Ø 7.2mm

56mm

13. Design drawing for Lalique 'Vibrante' pendant.

What is CAD?

Computer-aided design refers to any piece of software that can be used to design on a computer. This includes both two-dimensional (2D) and 3D design work. This is an intentionally wide definition, as there are dozens of different CAD software packages designed for specialist as well as general purposes.

CAD has had a significant impact on the jewellery industry. Such software allows the designer to demonstrate multiple perspectives and colour variations with ease. It's also useful for showing customers a prototype before a finished product is made and gives manufacturers a detailed technical specification from which to work. CAD isn't a substitute for traditional modes of design, but it is a useful, precision tool to aid the design process.

'Computer-aided design was originally built for creating perfect geometry for heavy industrial applications like aerospace and architecture. The fact that the tools have now become organic enough to be applied to forms of product design as organic as sculpture and jewellery design speaks volumes about not only how far computers have come in the past few decades but how advanced and intuitive the tools are becoming.'
Jack Meyer, Holts Academy of Jewellery, London

Design Creation

14–15. CAD visualization and rendering of a dragon egg in lead crystal and 18ct yellow gold.

14

15

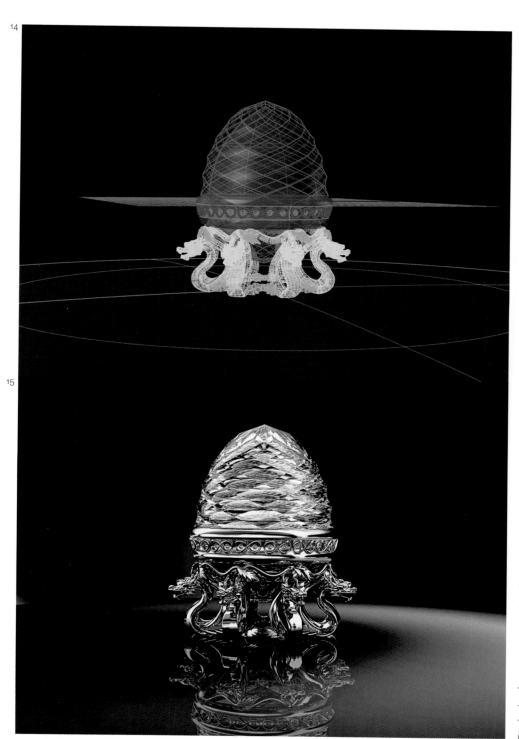

What is computer-aided manufacturing (CAM)?

Computer-aided manufacturing takes the objects created on-screen using CAD and turns them into real-world objects. There are many different types of technologies that use CAM; for example, the robotic arms used to assemble automobiles in car factories, and the small CNC milling machines that can carve tiny objects out of wax or metal.

Rapid prototyping is a special form of CAM designed to produce 'what you see is what you get' components, which precisely match the dimensions and measurements of 3D CAD-generated designs.

16. Rapid prototype machine printing.

17. CNC milling machines can accurately cut out small objects.

16

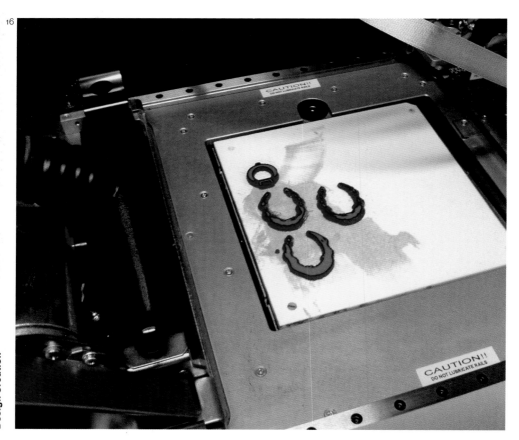

Design Creation

17

CAD

CAD software packages in jewellery design or manufacturing include the following.

2D design tools:
- Adobe Photoshop
- Corel Painter
- Gemvision Design
- Studio

2D vector drawing tools:
- Adobe Illustrator
- CorelDRAW
- Inkscape
- TypeEdit

3D model-making tools:
- 3DESIGN
- DelCAM PowerShape
- Gemvision Matrix
- Firestorm 3D CAD
- JewelCAD
- Monarch CAD
- Rhino (with either the Rhino Gold or Rhino Jewel plug-ins)

3D sculptural design tools:
- ArtCAM JewelSmith
- ClayTools
- Autodesk Mudbox
- ZBrush
  (3Design and Matrix also have built-in tools for handling some aspects of sculpture)

How does CAD apply to jewellery?

CAD's biggest advantage for jewellers is that designs can be tested before the piece is finished. If something needs to be changed, it can be modified much more quickly and cheaply in CAD than by handmade methods. In addition, thanks to rendering software, the designer can present a concept to a client that has not yet been realized. This allows the designer to sell designs and then manufacture on demand. Both of these combinations have helped bring bespoke design to a whole new market.

What does CAD do?

For all CAD's perfect precision, it still remains just a tool. It cannot design for you, nor can it serve as a short cut for producing good designs or well-made jewellery. Jewellers using CAD need to know just as much as a master goldsmith about how jewellery is made in order to effectively build their models.

18. 'Parametric' ring made with oxidized silver, designed by Sarah Herriot using CAD.

19. Bespoke gold-plated silver bangle inset with 185ct topaz, created by Sarah Herriot using CAD. The design is based on the structure of a crane.

19

18

Design Creation

How to get started with CAD

The best thing you can do to become a CAD jeweller is:

- Learn to draw: being able to develop your designs on paper is critical to any designer.

- Spend time hand-making metal or wax models at a bench: the more you've felt the materials the better you'll be at CAD.

Once you have developed these 'real world' skills, you're ready to get the most out of learning CAD. While it is definitely possible to learn CAD just by experimenting with a demo copy of the software, it is usually best to undertake a course, as it will give you somewhere to start. A good short course or CAD module as part of a degree course will go a long way.

20. 'Nouvelle Vague' a marcasite and silver bracelet designed by Joanna Dahdah for Swarovski Gem Visions 2012.

21. CAD drawing for Joanna Dahdah's 'Nouvelle Vague' bracelet.

21

20

Dorothée Pugnet is Head of Women's Jewellery & Accessories at Links of London.

22

22. Dorothée Pugnet
23. Dorothée Pugnet's personal 'Universe' moodboard documenting masculine and feminine themes.

Dorothée Pugnet started her career as a junior designer working on costume jewellery ranges at Dior when she was 21. But the story with Dior began much earlier when she secured a one-week internship working in their archives. From there she progressed from the archives to the studio, working on embroideries and doing everything from making coffee to textile experimentations.

She starts her collections by instinctively putting things together, such as pictures and materials. She has boxes full of objects found in flea markets or at suppliers. An important part of the process is creating moodboards and making collages, which help to keep her creative instinct sharp. Then she sketches many different ideas and starts to design only when she has enough material from which to choose a direction.

After drawing up the designs, Dorothée shares them with the product managers and developers to ensure that they fulfil the commercial needs of the brand. The collection is finalized at sample stage, by looking at the collection as a whole.

She works on several collections every year. Currently she works on a two-season basis, each season includes a brand new collection, some line extensions, plus some limited or seasonal animations.

Dorothée has, in the past, also worked for fashion houses. Then, she worked on four women's ready-to-wear collections, each comprising seven jewellery themes with between five to 25 pieces in each, plus two men's and two couture, and one cruise and one capsule (ski or Christmas).

Design Creation

One of the many challenges of working for a fashion house is keeping up with the fast pace of the fashion cycle, while working on several collections at the same time. It's also necessary to turn a creative brief (mainly words) into a successful product and match the creative director's vision. The biggest difference between a designer working for a brand and one working independently is finding the right balance between your own creative desires and what best suits the brand's DNA and market.

Dorothée has also gained experience from working as part of John Galliano's and Hedi Slimane's teams. She was able to see her designs mass-produced and distributed in different countries.

Her favourite designers are Riccardo Tisci for Givenchy and Alber Elbaz for Lanvin.

Dorothée feels that to succeed, young jewellery designers need to be curious, patient and ready to work hard for long hours. They should watch how more experienced people do things and learn from it. She advises designers to find their own world, as she says, 'You will always be asked to give a bit of yourself in everything you do'. And she feels it is important to do as many internships as possible, as it's the best school of life.

23

In large businesses, brand designers prepare their collections according to a range plan and critical path supplied by the business development team. The range plan details the retail and cost prices with which designs need to be aligned, the number of pieces required for a collection and the number of styles based on past performance, sales and market information. The range plan is a guide for the design team as to how many earrings, bracelets, necklaces and so on, a collection requires, to ensure that it stands the best possible chance of being a commercial success.

Editing is a natural part of the design process, regular reviews enable a designer to refine a collection and identify repetitive elements that need to be pared down, replaced or cut completely. There will inevitably be changes to styles, last-minute additions or modifications to materials for which the head of design and the creative director are ultimately responsible.

Regular reviews with the business development team and product managers ensure that a collection is on track, but even with careful planning the team will experience mistakes, delays and variables, and additional problems can occur with suppliers or freelance contractors.

24. Below are examples from Salima Thakker's 'Grid' collection, each point has been carefully mapped out: 18ct gold-plated cuff made with pearls and silver, designed by Salima Thakker.

25. 'Grid' 18ct white gold-plated cuff made with pearls and silver, designed by Salima Thakker.

26. 'Grid' 18ct white gold-plated cuff made with silver, designed by Salima Thakker.

24

Project management

It is a good idea for designers to draw up a timetable of works, where designs can be scheduled to meet the deadlines required to realize a finished piece. Creating a plan where key dates are highlighted enables designers to organize their time efficiently and manage the stages toward a finished collection. It is a good idea to build in time for unexpected delays.

Designers need to have an overview of how the whole project is coming together, to be prepared for hidden costs and technical difficulties. They may need to overcome challenges while preserving their creative vision and remaining flexible and adaptable throughout will help this process.

Reviewing

It is common for a creative director to reject ideas if they do not meet the creative vision. In the final stages, editorial considerations are based on the collection as a whole and how pieces sit together rather than as individual items. The creative director will review the collection with the team and has to ensure that there is no repetition, components and details are accurate and that there is the correct mix of daring and commercial.

Designers working as part of a team should be comfortable in presenting their ideas: a review with a head of design or creative director is a constructive dialogue, an exchange of ideas. Designers should be prepared to defend their design decisions and rationale. This is an evolutionary process and it is impossible to plan the entire process without revising and reworking ideas.

The final collection will then be signed off, which can involve a number of key people across the business including the CEO, creative director, head of merchandising, product development manager and head of business development.

25

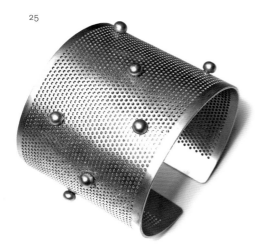

26

Maeve Gillies

27.

28.

27. Maeve Gillies

28. MaeVona's 'Eday' diamond ring set was awarded the JCK Jewelers' Choice Award in 2009 (US).

Maeve Gillies is president and chief creative officer of MaeVona a company that specializes in bridal and fashion jewellery with a Celtic twist.

Tell us about your background.

I started out on the bench at age 15. I then gained a BA Hons at ECA Edinburgh University and a Masters in Jewellery and Goldsmithing at the Royal College of Art, UK. I worked within jewellery around the world – as a designer, lecturer and manufacturing consultant – before spending three years as the head of design for Domino, the largest platinum jewellery manufacturer in Europe. I went on to launch my own business, MaeVona, in 2005, with my business partner in New York City.

You're originally from Scotland, how did you establish a brand in the US?

My co-founding business partner is American, and I had spent two years working in New York City as a fashion jewellery designer prior to my master's degree. This helped me to identify a niche in the American market for unique bridal designs with a Scottish heritage; I launched MaeVona specifically to fit this niche.

Why did you choose to establish a brand with a strong focus on bridal jewellery?

When I worked at Domino in England (a design company that is part of Weston Beamor, the UK's leading casting company) I had the challenge of adding fresh designs to a company catalogue with thousands of existing bridal designs. The impact on the European market that my designs had (5,000 customers in 30 countries) gave me confidence that I could do something special in this area. Also, I find bridal design very satisfying; I can spend a lot of time on attention to detail, creativity and craftsmanship, and due to the sentimental or symbolic value to the purchaser, this effort is truly appreciated.

What are the key design considerations for bridal?

Practicality: to be comfortable, durable and to protect the stone.

Elegance: to suit the hand and flatter the stone shape and wearer's finger.

Timeless design: creative and unique, yet classic enough not to date.

Design Creation

29

30

29. MaeVona's award-winning Celtic-inspired design drawings by Maeve Gillies.

30. 'Eorsa', 'Eriskay' and 'Scotasay' diamond rings designed by MaeVona.

How do materials influence your designs?

Precious materials inspire me, particularly a metal as rare and as special as platinum. How the object ages is also key for such an important jewel, as it will be worn daily for many years.

How does the American customer differ to the UK consumer?

Apart from differing in aesthetic choices, the major difference is in bridal buying habits – an American consumer will usually provide or select a diamond or gemstone first, then a mounting is chosen separately to fit. Also, branding is strong – an American consumer will research designer brands online and walk into a store to request a specific mounting or designer.

How many collections do you work on in a year?

Usually two bridal collections per year, and at least one fashion jewellery collection.

Do you work on any bespoke projects?

MaeVona creates custom versions of our existing designs, to fit customers' diamonds and gemstones. I also get involved with non-jewellery metal projects; for example, I created a limited edition silver whisky bottle for Highland Park Distillery's 50 year-old whisky that recently launched at Harrods (a luxury department store in London, UK) and won a Top 10 Packaging Design award in 2010.

What inspires you and how do you translate this into a design?

Love and life! Art and music, travel and nature, I translate all my thoughts into objects by drawing and refining on paper, then CAD.

What advice would you give a young designer?

Work hard, listen well. Be tenacious, gracious and vivacious. And once your designs sell, don't forget to keep evolving!

When planning and recording your work it is useful to have an initial range plan that details the number of pieces that you are making. Remember to include projected costings and wholesale and retail prices. This will give you a good overview of the whole project, its constraints, challenges and critical deadlines. It will also help you to identify any issues, hidden costs and areas that may need more research or sourcing of materials.

31

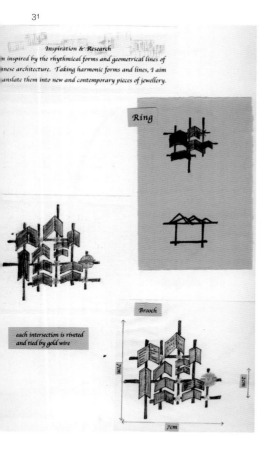

Inspiration & Research
...n inspired by the rhythmical forms and geometrical lines of
...nese architecture. Taking harmonic forms and lines, I aim
...anslate them into new and contemporary pieces of jewellery.

Ring

each intersection is riveted and tied by gold wire

Brooch

7cm

- Draw up a production chart or critical path for each piece in your collection. This will help you to manage your time efficiently and to identify key milestones.

- Keep a clear record of your work as you progress to help you to refine the collection and critique your own working practices.

- Maintain an archive of material explorations, technical drawings and anything else related to each design, so they can be rethought, experimented with and discussed post collection.

- Think about the functionality of the jewellery: is it designed for longevity, is it comfortable to wear, and is it attractive from every angle?

- Consider technical aspects, such as the practicalities of the design. For example, will a piece catch on clothing, is it too heavy to wear for long periods?

- Artistic consideration should be given to whether the design challenges traditional perceptions of jewellery. What reaction is it intended to create? Is the design innovative? Does it fulfil a niche in the market and how is it different to those of your competitors?

- Financially, remember to bear in mind which market you are aiming at and ensure that the price of the jewellery that you are designing will be appropriate for the target customer.

31–32. Pages from a student sketchbook and designs by BA student Mariko Sumioka, ECA, Edinburgh University, UK.

Design Creation

32

pilled up pieces and

up pieces with kimono......   good combination.....

Sterling silver 'Midas Touch'
necklace designed by
Elizabeth Galton.

This chapter explores how a collection is developed and comes to market. It looks at the people involved in the design team and explains their roles.

The lifecycle of manufacturing a brand collection is seasonal and dependent on numerous elements. It can take up to 12 months from initial sketch to the launch of a collection. Numerous factors are involved, including sampling, pricing and margin structures. The design team will collaborate with the teams responsible for the commercial side, visual merchandising and marketing needs of the business, as a collection progresses to the final stages of realization.

The development of a collection depends on a number of key team members who report to the creative director. The design team work alongside a studio manager, product development team or product development manager who is responsible for tracking the critical path of a collection, sourcing new suppliers or managing the existing supplier base.

1. The author and former creative director of Links of London, Elizabeth Galton, and photographer Peter Pedonomou art directing a photo shoot.

1

Creative director

The creative director leads the team, and he or she is responsible for setting the creative vision for the collection, from the initial design stages right through to sampling and manufacture. The creative director takes responsibility for decision-making and any amendments during the design process. The responsibility for ensuring the successful execution of the visual merchandising and marketing campaign may also fall to the creative director.

Briefing the design team and studio, and presenting collections to retail staff, is an important aspect of the role and the ability to communicate is as important as being creative. At this senior level, being business-minded is often the key to success.

Studio manager

In larger businesses, the design and product development teams may be co-ordinated by a studio manager. The studio manager liaises with the wider business teams or divisions, including marketing, merchandising and business development, who are responsible for co-ordinating marketing materials, product packaging, pack shots (photographs of products on a white background) and visual merchandising concepts.

Head of business development

The head of business development is responsible for co-ordinating the business development team, who conduct in-depth analysis of the market and identify the commercial needs of the business. Business development maps the range plan and sets the retail price for each collection, based on discussions with the retail and merchandising departments. This is then passed to the design team to execute. Business development is also responsible for liaising with the marketing department to agree all the materials required to market a collection, such as point-of-sale information, visual merchandising props, packaging and photography.

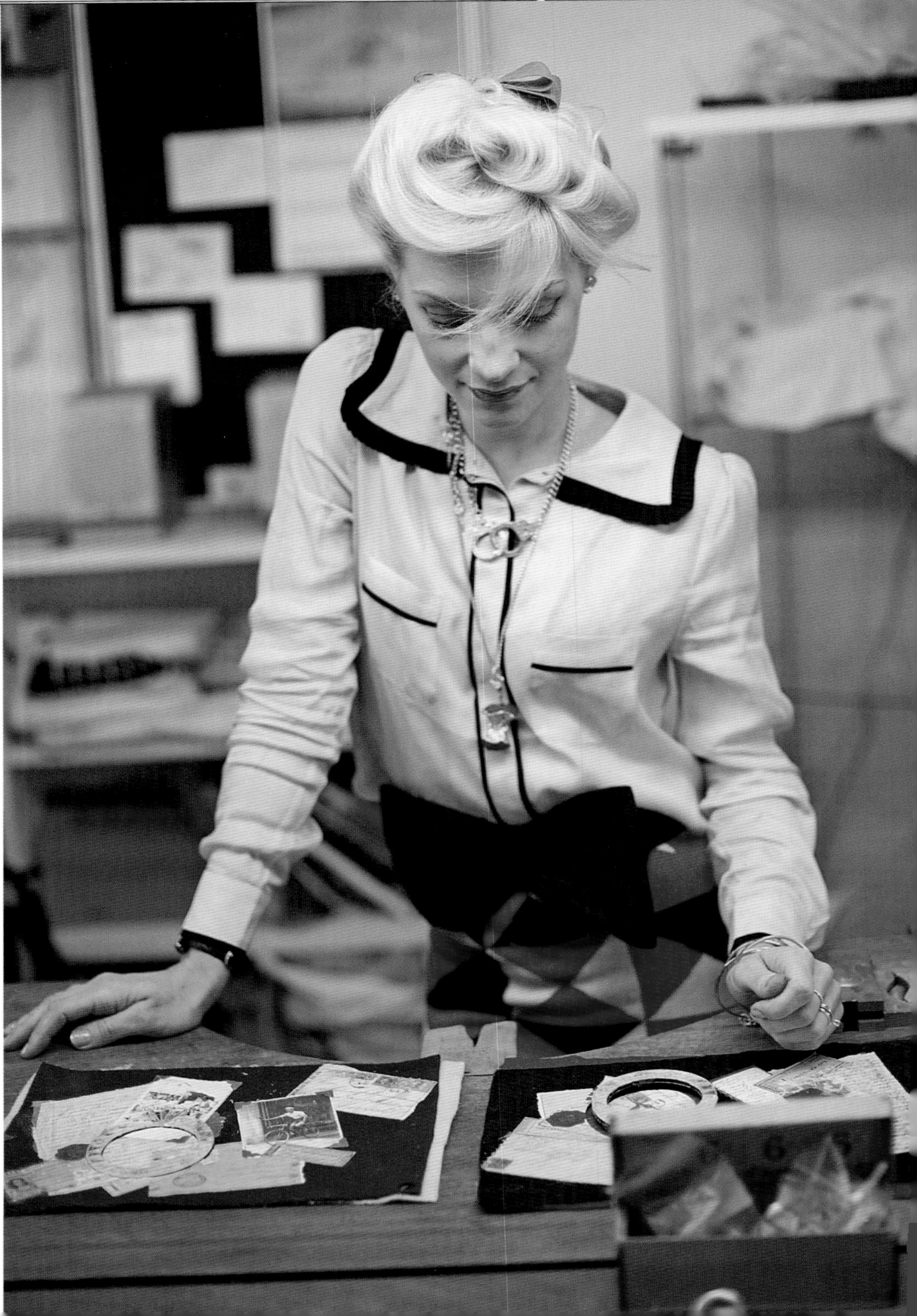

Head of design

In the largest jewellery brands, it is usual to have senior design positions with responsibility for very specific product areas, such as men's jewellery and watches or women's jewellery. These designers are also responsible for managing junior designers on a day-to-day basis.

Product developer

The product developer tracks the critical path of a product, ensuring designs are realized according to the design teams requirements and the creative director's original vision. A product developer sources new suppliers, obtains materials and findings for a collection and manages existing suppliers.

Model maker/prototype maker

Large brands will often retain the services of an experienced craftsperson to work on initial prototypes and models. This enables the design team to see results quickly and make adjustments prior to the collection being briefed to the manufacturer.

CAD designer

Design teams are often supported by a senior designer experienced in CAD design; necessary for detailed specifications and complex projects.

Resources

A typical start-up design business may well be located in an independent or shared workshop, the latter making it possible for a designer to rent a bench space. Basic equipment in a shared workshop includes a bench, polishing mop, guillotine, rolling mill, torch and hearth (forge), and a small pickle tank for cleaning metal. A space for conducting meetings with visitors is also beneficial and lends a professional air.

Depending on how a collection is made and the budget available, it is common practice to outsource specialist activities to outworkers such as setters, engravers, polishers, platers and casters for which costs must be carefully managed.

2. British designer Jessica de Lotz at work in her London studio. She is is a typical example of a young, successful start-up business and burgeoning brand.

3

3. Theo Fennell

4

4. *Dum Spiro Spero* (While I breathe, I hope) pendant made with 9.40ct green tourmaline, from Fennell's *Carpe Diem* collection.

Jewellery and silver designer Theo Fennell has a star-studded client roster that includes the late Elizabeth Taylor, Elton John, Ozzy Osbourne and Lady Gaga. Theo opened his first fine jewellery store above his studio and workshop in Chelsea, London, in 1982, and boutiques in prestigious department stores such as Harrods, Selfridges and Harvey Nichols followed.

The Theo Fennell brand is famous for witty, quirky and beautifully made jewellery and hand-crafted silverware that includes, luxury takes on great British culinary staples such as solid silver Marmite lids, ketchup holders and a chip fork and pieces engraved with *sic transit gloria mundi* – 'thus passes the glory of the world'.

Why did you choose jewellery as a career?

My family were all in the military, so this was quite a departure. I went to art school, as art institutions were bursting with ideas in the 1970s, and did portraiture. After I left I was, by chance, offered job in a silversmiths and fell in love with the whole tradition of collective work, detailed design and craftsmanship.

What is your design ethos and signature style?

I believe jewellery and silver should really mean something and be made for eternity – not a statement of wealth or fashion. It is a deeply emotional thing and, as such, should be invested with great design and craftsmanship. I think style is a sense rather than a feature. I believe in keeping one's eyes and brain open to all influences and ideas. That designs can be cerebral or visual, as classical or quirky as one likes. But they must end up being believable. Sentimental or humorous, they must still resonate and I don't think a 'look' always does this.

5

5. Antique poison bottle with silver stopper, designed by Theo Fennell.

6

6. Theo Fennell's themes are often dark and romantic, with *memento mori* skull references, as with this ring.

How does a collection evolve, what is the starting point?

It can be anything. A chance remark, a glimpsed detail on a building, a song, a book, a naked body or a squashed insect – not all references are visual. Then it is a question of sketching and seeing where it leads. Just sometimes, a design comes fully formed into my mind.

How do you go about designing a diffusion collection while retaining the signature style of your exclusive pieces?

Make sure it is beautifully made and that you do not patronize the people you are designing for just because it is less expensive.

What constitutes good jewellery design?

That it fulfils its original intention using the best materials and crafted in the best way possible to achieve that end. Then it should become a talismanic part of its owner's life.

How are your collections made?

I have both a terrific studio team and an excellent workshop full of brilliant craftsmen. Some have been with me over 25 years. They are from 17 to 70, so there is a fantastic spectrum of experience and enthusiasm. From the basic concept it can sometimes be just me sitting down with one craftsman that I have worked with for years or else a truly 'repertory' effort, a collective of sympathetic minds and talents to make something – rather like a miniature cathedral, combining many skills.

What do you look for in a young designer?

Humour, an inquisitive and open mind, enthusiasm, talent and above all, tenacity. They must want to design jewellery with the desperation that an actor wants to act or a ballet dancer wants to dance. It is not for the spoilt or faint-hearted.

A supplier and materials database can be built up via trade shows and industry contacts and work placements. Many of the industry's governing bodies have directories, which a designer can buy or access to source reputable suppliers. While the bigger manufacturers and Asian suppliers have large minimum order quantities, it is possible to negotiate smaller production runs with local manufacturers. Many Asian suppliers have international agents based in Western markets who can oversee production for designers unable to make regular trips to Asia.

The manufacturing process also employs specialist suppliers or artisans for specialist techniques, and local or European factories will undertake small-batch production runs. Most major cities have jewellery districts where suppliers are based, such as Hatton Garden in London (UK), Birmingham's Jewellery Quarter (UK) and the Diamond District in New York City (USA) located at West 45th–48th Street between Fifth Avenue and Seventh Avenue, which is one of the primary centres of the global diamond industry.

7. Silver is hallmarked by an Assay Office to show that it reaches the required legal standard of silver content.

7

8

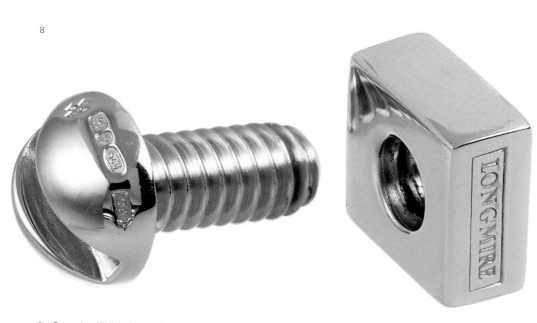

8. 'Screw' cufflink by Longmire: the silver hallmark can be seen on top of the screw.

Hallmarking

Hallmarking is unique to the jewellery, goldsmithing and silversmithing industry. A hallmark is an official mark or series of marks struck on items made of precious metals. Hallmarks are a guarantee of certain purity or fineness of the metal, as determined by formal metal (assay) testing. Historically, hallmarks were applied by a trusted party: the 'guardians of the craft' or nowadays by an Assay Office.

The UK's Assay Offices are located in London, Edinburgh, Sheffield and Birmingham. To be a true hallmark, it must be the guarantee of a recognized independent body or authority that the contents are as marked.

The control or inspection of precious metals was an ancient concept of examination and marking, by means of inspection stamps (punch marks). The use of hallmarks, at first on silver, has a long history dating back to the fourth century AD and represents the oldest known form of consumer protection.

Designers and brands will also have their own 'maker's mark' (or logo) to distinguish their products from that of other designers and brands. These makers' marks accompany the hallmark and generally last for ten years. Hallmarks are offered in the form of a punch or as a laser mark, suitable for more delicate jewellery pieces, which cannot be struck.

A designer may also hold a brand trademark, which can be registered via the Patent Office as a means of protecting the brand name in different countries.

Designers working for an established brand follow a range plan to ensure that they are designing a piece that meets the commercial requirements of the business. An experienced designer will be aware of the cost of raw materials, target cost price and the margins their designs need to meet. A business will identify the retail pricing of its competitors and what the market will bear, based on sales and past performance.

9. 'Dragonfly' bangle set with green tourmaline, star sapphire, aquamarine, moonstone, blue topaz, indigolite and diamonds, from Boodles.

9

A new designer can use 'competitor shops' to research competitors at the market level that they wish to target. If there are no competitors, a visit to a high-quality department store or boutique will show you how market-level definitions are defined by retailers.

Retailers and department stores may mark up a designer's wholesale price by up to 300 per cent of the wholesale price. This mark up is referred to as the 'triple key' or 'triple keystone'. Fine jewellery collections can cost a huge amount of money to produce, but this is not a prerequisite to success, and many jewellers enter the market with a small collection of key pieces that can be expanded upon as they grow their stockist and client base.

Retailers make more profit than the designer because they have to cover their staffing costs, advertising and promotion, sales duties, rent and overheads. Unlike some other commercial products, jewellery commands a high margin due to its intrinsic value and the skill involved in producing it.

Costings

It is important to be realistic when planning and costing a collection, and it should reflect your chosen market and customer.

In order to arrive at a 'cost price' or 'cost of goods', a designer calculates the amount of time it takes to make a piece, the cost of all the materials, any outsourced work such as plating and casting, and finally hallmarking. This figure does not include research and development – time spent coming up with a design – since this would make the piece financially unviable; this may be written off (amortized) over time. One-off pieces are always more expensive as their set-up costs cannot be written off over a period and they are often made using intensive methods. Whereas repetitive runs or editions of a design have economies of scale built into their production.

Large-scale production of jewellery involves batch production techniques such as casting, electroforming or stamping, which makes repetition of them faster and more efficient.

In order to calculate a 'wholesale price' (the price the designer gives retailers), the designer will add a mark up of up to 100 per cent to the cost price; this is the 'profit margin'. The profit margin is the amount by which revenue from sales exceeds costs in a business before tax.

It is a good exercise to use a similar product made by a competitor as a benchmark for price. Take the retail price and work backwards to see realistically what cost price you will need to try and achieve. Based on this, you can assess whether a product is commercially viable.

Materials and sourcing > **Pricing designs** > Sampling

The sampling process links the design and manufacture processes, samples are made up either by a model maker, in-house craftsman or factory (depending on the size of a business) to ensure a designer's vision is carried through to manufacture and then to the shop floor.

The first set of samples may be reworked and sometimes materials are substituted if the cost is too high after the margins are added. The design team will then receive a final set of 'production samples' for sign-off by the wider business and these will then go into production.

10. Wax is often used to create prototypes. Lalique 'Serpent' pendant wax prototype; the motif is a symbol of luck.

Design Development and Realization

11. Lalique 'Serpent' pendant based on the 'Sacred Fire Odyssey – Fauna of Fire' theme. Made with yellow gold, lacquer, tassels and amber crystal. Limited edition of ten pieces created for the Chinese New Year.

Key materials

What is yellow gold?

Gold is graded by carat (ct) in the UK, in the US by karat (k). The carat system for gold, unlike diamonds, is a measure of the purity of gold by weight. The carat measures the proportion of gold to other metals in a particular alloy. Pure gold is 24 carat; 22 carat gold contains 22 parts of gold to two parts of other metals; 18 carat gold contains 18 parts of gold to six parts of other metals and is thus 75 per cent pure gold. While nine-carat gold contains nine parts of gold to 15 parts of other metals.

The colour of pure gold is a vivid metallic yellow. However, copper and silver are the principal metals used for gold alloy, though zinc, cadmium, iron and aluminium are also used. The refiner's problem is to reach a satisfactory compromise between working qualities and colour for each different carat quality.

What is white gold?

White gold is achieved by combining pure gold with alloys such as silver and palladium. Traditionally, nickel was used in white gold; however, nickel is no longer used in most modern white gold as it can cause allergic reactions in some wearers.

As the natural colour of white gold is a greyish colour, almost all white gold jewellery is plated with a metal called rhodium, which is a member of the platinoid family of metals. Rhodium is used to brighten the colour of white gold.

12. 'Midas Touch' orchid ring for 'Cool Diamonds', made with 18ct white gold and diamonds, designed by Elizabeth Galton.

12

13

13. Award-winning design for the Diamond International Necklace (watercolour on tinted paper). The design features black, gold-plated snake chain, side clips set with navettes and baguettes, and tassels set with brilliants, tapered baguettes and navettes, designed by Jocelyn Burton for De Beers.

14. Design for a necklace made with carved black onyx, black, gold-plated 18 ct gold snake chain and mixed diamonds (watercolour on paper, 1999), designed by Jocelyn Burton for De Beers.

14

What is rose gold?

Rose gold is the result of varying the proportions of copper and silver in the alloy, which results in a beautiful reddish-pink hue.

What is sterling silver?

Sterling silver is an alloy of silver containing 92.5 per cent by mass of silver and 7.5 per cent by mass of other metals, usually copper. The sterling silver standard is 925 parts per thousand. As pure silver is generally too soft for manufacturing into larger objects and for everyday wear, copper is generally used to give it strength while at the same time preserving the ductility of the metal and its beauty. The presence of copper is also the reason why silver tends to oxidize or tarnish.

What is vermeil?

Vermeil is a term that is most often used in the fashion-led jewellery market. Vermeil is a combination of sterling silver with a layer of gold on top. To be considered vermeil, the gold must be at least 10 ct and be at least 1.5 micrometres thick. Any other metal plated onto sterling silver cannot be called vermeil. Vermeil can be produced by fire gilding or eletrolytic plating. Fire gilding is an antiquated process, however, and most vermeil these days is produced by way of electrolysis. Vermeil is a French word, now commonly used in the English language, mostly in America. It became a popular term in the nineteenth century as an alternative to the term 'silver-gilt'.

15

16

15. 'Hart 'Art' pendant made with rose gold, ruby and diamonds, designed by Theo Fennell.

16. 'Coronet' ring made with yellow gold, citrine, diamonds and sapphire, designed by Theo Fennell.

Pricing designs > Sampling > Case study: Product development

17

18

17. 'AD Vintage Logo' cufflinks for Dunhill made with brass and platinum plated, inspired by branding first used in the early 1900s.

18. 'Rotating Lighthouse' cufflinks for Dunhill, made with solid 18ct pink gold, containing 48 champagne diamonds set in a rotating mechanism.

Chris Tague works in product development. He has worked for Dunhill and Links of London.

Chris did a degree in Management Science (Business) at Loughborough University with a year's industry placement (with Reebok).

On graduating, he secured a student placement with Dunhill, assisting with sample development, quality control and the product development of jewellery, watches, gifts, pens and lighters. He then went to work in the gift division as a junior product manager, working on a wider number of products including cufflinks. He was with Dunhill for four years and then moved on to Links of London.

Product developers often work with an overseas sourcing office; they format designs to include specs, costs and timeline targets and agree when samples will be available.

Since most product developers work with Asia, they have to manage the time zone difference efficiently. An average day starts with dealing with email queries from suppliers to make sure products are on track. Then liaising with different departments, including preparing sign-offs for products, answering designers' queries, providing samples to marketing for photo shoots or meeting with merchandising to present products so that they can start preparing their buys.

When working with jewellery designers, it is important to manage their expectations. Communication is critical at the outset, giving designers feedback as to what is feasible or cost prohibitive. A good product developer won't make decisions on behalf of designers, but will ensure that the designers have enough input so that when the product arrives they know what to expect.

Design Development and Realization

19

19. The iconic high jewellery house of Boucheron can still be found in the Place Vendôme in Paris. Boucheron was founded in 1858 and is now owned by the Gucci Group.

Nathalie Mallet has worked with Boucheron and is collections manager at Links of London.

Nathalie Mallet attended a French business school where she specialized in product marketing.

She began her career at Boucheron in Paris, France on a one-year internship, starting in merchandising and then in high jewellery marketing. Being part of the product team enabled her to discover all the stages in the development of new collections: from the commercial brief, to the research, hand-drawings, sourcing stones from around the world and the development in the Parisian workshops, in Place Vendôme.

The collections manager's role is to brief the designers, follow up the project and make sure that the workload in the studio is running smoothly.

As collections manager for Links of London, Nathalie works closely with the design team on a daily basis. She manages the briefs and timelines in the studio, meaning that she is the key contact for the designers.

Nathalie has learned to work with each designer slightly differently; she has to remain firm on the priorities, and also be very diplomatic.

Nathalie has regular catch-ups with the design team to discuss current and future briefs, review designs in progress and agree sign-off timelines.

20

21

22

21–22. 'Large Weight' pendant and 'Large Weight' ring made from sterling silver and plated with 18 ct rose gold, designed by Kasia Piechocka.

20. Kasia Piechocka in her workshop.

Kasia Piechocka is a recent graduate, who is trying to establish her own brand.

How are you finding life in the industry since graduation?

Life as a new designer in the industry is extremely challenging and competitive! However, I think my organized and professional approach – even while studying at Central Saint Martins, London, UK – has meant that the transition into the industry has not been as painful as it has been for some of my colleagues.

The current economic climate makes it difficult to set up any brand, let alone a luxury one. Meticulous long-term planning and a strong determination to succeed help you to adapt to the industry.

Have you been working as an intern or doing other work to support yourself while you establish your brand?

I've taken a long-term approach towards the development of my brand; gaining a reputation as a unique, high-quality designer is of greater importance to me. To enable me to build up a sustainable brand, I've chosen to work two part-time jobs as well as being self-employed. This means that I don't rely on income from my jewellery, and can invest the money that I make from it straight back into the business. At the moment I'm working for jewellery brand Hannah Martin Ltd a few days a week as well as part-time in a restaurant. I also work from my studio on bespoke pieces and other special orders for individual customers.

How have you found getting your work seen by buyers and stockists?

I have found that the vast majority of buyers take an interest in seeing the professionalism and quality of work produced by a CSM graduate. Cash flow is the biggest barrier when trying to retail my jewellery.

Design Development and Realization

23

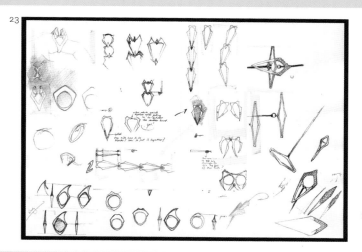

23. Kasia Piechocka's sketchbook work from the collection 'About the Man Who Loved Fishing'.

Most stockists are not currently investing in fine jewellery stock. As a young brand, my stock is made to order, it's not possible for me to self-finance stock for boutiques. This current inability to stock on a 'sale or return' basis means that I am somewhat restricted in the number of stockists I can approach.

Have you found it easy to get your work seen by magazines and blogs?

I think any new brand faces difficulty getting significant interest from magazines. As I have discovered, they are often much more interested in featuring established names and rather reluctant to feature smaller, lesser known brands. It is very much a 'chicken and egg' situation with magazines and stockists. Magazines only seem to want to feature products stocked by big retailers, and stockists want to sell products that have had a lot of press coverage! I've found working with bloggers a simpler process as they have more freedom to write about whatever they want.

Any tips for new graduates based on your experiences?

I would advise soon-to-be graduates not to simply listen and follow all the advice you are given; but to apply them to your ideas, plans and way of working. Advice should be looked at as a tool to help you to succeed, not as a guide on how to succeed.

Talk to people and be open about what you are doing. Most of all, I think it is extremely important to be focused. You need to be 100 per cent committed to succeed and be prepared to work very hard.

What has been the most exciting aspect of your flourishing career?

My lifelong dream was not only to be an artist, but also to be able to showcase my work and make a living out of it. It's exhilarating for me to see my brand growing, developing and steadily approaching the point where it can financially support me. Starting up with little experience and capital is a difficult path to take; but it makes it more satisfying when you do reach the milestones.

The realization of design ideas involves material experimentation, sample creation and production. You may explore specialist techniques such as enamelling, fold forming, engraving, etching and electroforming to see which processes best suit your ideas and designs.

By this stage of the process, you should be sourcing stones, suitable fastenings and chains, and ordering metals. You might be working with outworkers such as casters, platers and stone setters. You should be following your critical path and range plan to ensure that you are on track and anticipating any issues that may arise, revising and reworking designs accordingly.

■ Research suitable fastenings, chains, stones and metals and consider how and where your designs may be worn.

■ Think about the clothing your pieces will be worn with and their potential weight. Consider how easy the designs will be to put on without assistance and how long they will be worn for.

■ Discuss your ideas with experienced makers, setters and platers to ensure that you haven't missed any technical issues.

24

24. 'Green Eye Fish Head' ring made with oxidized sterling silver and emeralds, designed by Kasia Piechocka.

25

- Compile your research into a series of categories – inspiration, colours and stones, materials and texture explorations. Next, create CAD drawings or technical from which to create initial samples in metal or wax.

- Do some sample experiments, for example use a rolling mill to try out textures on flat metal. Enamel test pieces or experiment with wax carving tools or electroforming and casting techniques. Stakes, hammers and doming punches may also be used to create shapes.

- Use drawings and photographs as an easy visual resource to explore ideas and permutations.

- It is important to remain flexible and open to change, as ideas may not work as you expect, or the availability of materials may change.

25. Sketchbook work from Kasia Piechocka's collection 'About the Man Who Loved Fishing'.

'Vertical Veil' headpiece designed
by Philip Treacy for Swarovski
Runway Rocks made with
Swarovski Elements.

Today jewellery brands sell products using sophisticated images, campaigns and styling transmitted through a wealth of media including flagship stores, pop-up shops, digital magazines, online stores, web films, apps and virtual fashion shows.

In the last decade, the Internet, mass media and the expansion of brands into new, emerging economies has led to the development of a very savvy consumer. Online shopping and social media have seen shopping become a truly social experience and the wealth and breadth of goods available has exploded. Online shopping allows consumers to compare retail outlets across a vast number of products, which means companies need to be clever when presenting their goods. They do this by consistently reinforcing their unique brand proposition and catering to the interests and needs of their customer.

Branding is a powerful tool and even the smallest brand or designer needs to carefully build a unique visual identity in order to succeed in such a fast-paced, high-tech environment. In this chapter, we look at the key building blocks for presenting and promoting a collection to consumers, buyers and the press.

A lookbook is a commercial photographic record documenting a collection, which the designer compiles each season to present the collection to retailers and press. The books are designed to assist buyers and editors in making their choices and to inform their in-store merchandise stories and displays. Pictures are usually 'pack shots' (products photographed on a white background) and may be accompanied with a few key editorial shots (on models). The book will also include details about pricing, materials and contact information and press coverage at the back (similar to a line sheet).

Established brands present glossy hard copies, but if budget does not permit, a lookbook can be presented digitally in the form of a PDF. The lookbook should be clear and informative and not overly fussy. A designer should consider the styling and total look they wish to convey when preparing a lookbook. The theme of the collection, whether whimsical, quirky, dramatic and dark, or humorous, will be reflected with the use of relevant props and models.

1. Editorial shot from the lookbook for the 'Orchid Collection', designed by Elizabeth Galton.

A portfolio will ultimately secure you a job or placement with a designer or company and it needs to create an impact. Employers look for graduates who have the ability to demonstrate an understanding of the stages of design through to the final execution of a collection.

Your portfolio should demonstrate that you are capable of assessing trends, are knowledgeable about key influencers working in the industry, as well as showing your creative diversity. It should be carefully edited and separated into six to eight projects demonstrating your approach to technical drawings, IT applications, visual research and material explorations.

It should also illustrate an awareness of your competitors and that you have undertaken market-based studies and identified your customer. Look at how brands layout their catalogues and lookbooks for inspiration, since this will inform your methodology and approach to 2D imagery as part of your portfolio.

Portfolio dos and don'ts

Do...

- Ensure that the work in your portfolio is suitable for the company that will be interviewing you or you will be presenting to, rather than taking a 'one size fits all' approach.

- Check and double-check every detail.

- Be consistent with presentation formats within a project, ensure everything is well mounted, legible and titled correctly.

- Invest in good-quality images to showcase work as professionally as possible.

- Ensure that you keep your portfolio manageable and up-to-date, and be prepared to reconfigure it depending on the type of interview.

Don't...

- Be tempted to include everything; edit your portfolio carefully and show only your strongest body of work.

- Use plastic bags when presenting your jewellery samples; these can be slow and time consuming to unpack. It is worth investing in a specialist jewellery roll or box.

- Include something in your portfolio with which you are unhappy or unconfident about – it is never good practice to be apologetic or embarrassed during an interview.

Some designers will opt to present their portfolio in digital format, but remember that the viewer will be unable to touch or feel the jewellery as part of the viewing. It does, however, allow a designer to present to a larger audience and means that the portfolio is immediately accessible to companies and recruiters globally. Digital presentations have really changed the face of job-hunting for a new generation of designers. However, some companies may wish to see a hard copy of the portfolio in addition to a laptop presentation and it is wise to have one since this allows for the computer crashing, batteries dying and other such eventualities.

Potential employers will look to see if interviewees have researched their business and know key facts about their market and customers. A candidate is more likely to stand out from other candidates if they have produced a short research and design project tailored to the company. This demonstrates that the candidate is enthusiastic and has taken time to prepare specifically for the interview.

Portfolio contents

A portfolio should include:

1 A CV/résumé directed at the job applied for. This should be no longer than two pages and start with your most recent achievements or position.

2 A covering letter, addressed to the person interviewing you, in case the portfolio is asked for in advance of an interview.

3 A design or artist's statement. This should detail your design approach.

4 The brief for each project.

5 Design sketches and research from your sketchbooks.

6 Technical or CAD drawings.

7 Moodboards.

8 Industry or trend research.

9 Finished presentation drawings.

10 Labelled samples.

11 Images of prototypes and finished pieces.

12 Photographs of the pieces being worn.

13 Final lookbook.

14 Press clippings (if you have them).

15 Business cards.

Photographs are used as a selling tool. It is important that a designer has a set of high-resolution 'pack shot' product images photographed on a plain white background to supply to buyers and press. Today, many magazines will ask the designer to supply still-life images of a product for inclusion in their shopping pages and without these a designer may miss a valuable publicity opportunity. Still-life shots are product-focused, while editorial shots focus on a more conceptual or surreal approach where an image conveys the story or advertising message. An independent designer or smaller brand needs to employ expertise and flair in presenting their brand and products to their full advantage.

Photographs should include close-up shots of the product's fastenings or catches and showcase the product from different angles. It is important to ensure that images are well lit, pin sharp, to scale and accurately representative of the product's stone or metal colour. It can be tempting to render designs using computer packages rather than actual photographs, but this is never particularly effective.

3

2

2. Close-up shot of 'Mohawk' cocktail ring made with 18ct white gold, diamonds and Tahitian pearl, designed by Andrew Geoghegan.

3. Elizabeth Galton's 'Ampura' pendant from the *cabinet de curiosité* collection is photographed on a white background.

4. The cover of the lookbook *cabinet de curiosité* with its clean lines and white background reflects the type of photography recommended for showing designs.

5. Elizabeth Galton's silver and amethyst charm bracelet from the *cabinet de curiosité* collection. The pin sharp photograph reveals the delicacy of the design.

4

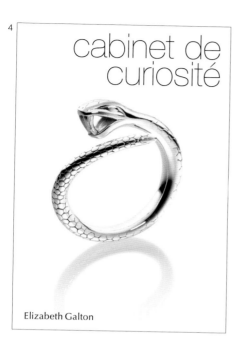

cabinet de
curiosité

Elizabeth Galton

Editorial or campaign shots may also be used by a designer depending on their resources. These will be styled according to the designer's creative vision and offer the opportunity for a more flamboyant approach. The tone of the images will mirror the story of the collection – whether it is inspired by a particular location, object or theme – and will use models and props accordingly.

Making connections with other upcoming professionals, such as stylists and photographers, is often a good way to get a collection photographed on a budget. Such professionals will have access to 'new faces' (young models) who need shots for their own portfolios and their agencies are therefore often willing to accept a significantly reduced rate, if not work for free.

5

Today, it is not merely enough for designers to be talented artists, they must have a firm grasp on how their products will be marketed and how to create a story and a USP (unique selling proposition) around their product, achieving a balance between design flair and the commercial aspects necessary to achieve an enduring success.

Brands spend significant sums of money creating, maintaining and protecting their brand identity. The brand name or logo is the single most valuable and powerful asset a company has at its disposal. Brand identities need to engage with consumers on several levels: personal, emotional and functional. The strongest brands capture the consumers' attention with their look and their unique personalities, they impress with their heritage and magnetism.

The brand identity differentiates the brand from their competitors and may be made up of a number of marks and colour variations. The most iconic logos are immediately recognizable globally and consumers connect with them and make particular assumptions, without necessarily seeing the product. Logos may also be used as a repeat pattern on a product and used on hardware and fastenings (findings), or be synonymous with a particular product.

6. Louis Vuitton's iconic monogram and branding is recognized the world over.

7. Dunhill use their logo as a signature detail on their products.

8. High jewellery house Boucheron create memorable campaigns for their 'hero products'.

9. Sapphire and diamond panther clip by Cartier crouched on a large cabochon sapphire. The panther motif is synonymous with the Cartier brand.

8

9

'The brand story is about the artist, his creative universe, his beliefs and values as well as technique, materials and all the emotional touch-points that the work may evoke. The less it touches us emotionally, the less we may be interested in it. A human being has many stories to tell, as should a brand.'
Philippe Mihailovich,
Professor of Luxury Brand
Management at EDHEC
Business School, France

Building a brand

10

Creating a brand can be done gradually and even with a limited budget. Regardless of the available budget attention to every small detail – be it packaging, product care cards, or press releases – is critical in order to stand out from the crowd.

A small brand or designer can work with a graphic designer to create a simple representation of a logo. It is also worthwhile spending some time choosing a name that is memorable. A brand name can be trademarked in a designer's home country and in the overseas markets in which it intends to trade; this should be considered a mid to long-term investment since it can be extremely costly.

Many packaging suppliers can be commissioned to supply small batch runs of logo packaging or off-the-shelf packaging can be sourced and customized and upgraded as a brand grows.

11

12

10. Jessica De Lotz's flat-pack 'Pressie in the post' ring reflects her quirky, handmade designs and highly personal service.

11. The packaging of William Cheshire's 'Libertine' pendant has a unique tag line – 'escape from the politely organized' – that captures the spirit of the brand.

12. Allumer has created a distinctive brand identity around the French word *allumer* meaning 'to light up', which has a synergy with their 'Match Royal' necklace.

13. SHO Fine Jewellery packaging is distinctive and luxurious in keeping with the brand's ethos.

13

Starting a brand

When building a brand from scratch consider the following:

- How well does the name lend itself to appearing on packaging?

- Can the brand name be abbreviated into a logo?

- How memorable is the brand name, is it easily pronounceable for different nationalities?

- Is it synonymous with the market level you intend to target?

- Is the brand colour masculine or feminine and appropriate for the consumer it is intended for?

- What does the brand name convey: is it humorous, luxurious, and eponymous (i.e. your name)?

- Are there relevant Internet URLs available to purchase including .com, .net , co.uk, .co?

- Has the name already been trademarked?

Brands and designers employ public relations (PR) agencies to promote their brands to journalists and editors, ensuring a consistent message is maintained and conveyed in the press. PR agents will promote designers to bloggers, stylists and their editorial and celebrity clients. If a high-profile celebrity wears a piece of jewellery on TV or to a red carpet event, the PR representative can generate free press (free publicity) for the designer or brand by promoting the fact that the celebrity is endorsing the product, either officially or unofficially. This type of promotion is valuable for a young designer who cannot afford forms of paid advertising, since such celebrity images are invariably picked up by the style press and can set a designer on a significant career trajectory.

14

WWW.ALLUMER.CO.UK
COPYRIGHT OF NATASHA LEITH-SMITH AND ALLUMER

15

The role of the PR agent is to be press facing, preparing and disseminating brand news. This takes the form of press releases on new collections, coordinating new launches, press shows and press appointments around the year – feeding the media with relevant stories and samples. Individual brands may engage a PR consultant on an ad-hoc basis rather than a monthly retainer and some PR consultants may also act as sales agents, introducing designers to relevant retailers.

14. Allumer's website shows examples of where their jewellery has been featured in magazines and photo shoots.

15. A publicity picture promoting one of William Cheshire's jewellery designs showcasing his brand's provocative and edgy style.

Tips for emerging designers

Many young designers promote products themselves, without the aid of a PR representative. In such instances, blogs and social media are a valuable resource and designers should ensure that they are present on as many community platforms as possible, such as Twitter, Fashiolista and Facebook. Many magazine editors are open to being approached directly, though perseverance is required and bloggers are often a good choice since they are always keen to discover new talent.

Blogger outreach has become 'the new PR'. Reasons to reach out to bloggers:

- trust – consumers trust the endorsements of respected bloggers and are more likely to purchase work recommended by them;

- cost effective – it only takes time and effort to get your brand noticed by most bloggers, rather than the financial resources required by more traditional advertising routes;

- measurable ROI (return on investment) – you can quickly see the effect blogger outreach has on sales;

- potential to go viral – respected bloggers' tips are often passed on to a wider audience via community platforms and style forums, giving your designs more exposure.

When loaning jewellery to the press, designers should ensure that they issue a loan form to the magazine, detailing the piece and its wholesale value and this requires a signature from the magazine on delivery; this is important for high-ticket items in the event of a piece going missing or being lost on a shoot. Some magazines will provide a PR agent with credit card details as insurance, but designers should ensure that insurance is in place for valuable pieces.

Social media

Social media is a powerful tool for establishing an audience for any brand, and large companies now make significant investments in this marketing medium. Social media can be likened to the coffee shop opposite your store.

However, having a Facebook page or Twitter feed in itself is not the barometer for success. It's the continued engagement with the audience that will dictate the effect social media plays for any business. Anyone can develop interesting, shareable, and most importantly, easy content for social media, but it tales time and commitment.

Tips for building an online audience

1   Brands should consider using Facebook to engage with the customer: ask questions, run polls and competitions.

2   Share anything 'behind the scenes', show the people behind the brand. This is an opportunity to be less formal than with traditional marketing methods.

3   Ask your customers, fans or followers for feedback.

4   Report live from an event.

5   Share inspiring content and professional tips with others.

6   Pull out something from the archives.

7   Host an online event.

8   Don't forget the power of the press – use your coverage.

9   'Top 10 Best of Lists' are always popular with consumers.

Marketing

Websites

Before the success of e-commerce, it was thought that consumers would never spend money on luxury goods online. We now know this is not the case. The wealth and breadth of luxury goods has exploded and comparison shopping is a top utility of online shopping. As a result, big and small brands need an online presence.

The Internet is a valuable tool for redefining the luxury and fashion jewellery shopping experience, since it presents an opportunity to reach customers directly and build brand loyalty. In fashion, the online retail revolution is having an impact with online catwalk; traditional live runway shows are being replaced with virtual runway fashion shows, iPad magazines and Facebook live-streams. Mobile tagging augmented reality applications and 3D films are also advancing, and brands are investing heavily in this high-tech world.

Graduates looking to establish their own independent practice should aim to have a web presence at the time of their graduate show: this can comprise a simple landing page with contact details, or if budget permits a product portfolio, blog and professional credentials, which can be expanded. Today, an online presence is critical and presents the opportunity to capture customers directly who can then be retained by simple marketing tactics, such as special offers, competitions, blog updates and newsletter communications.

16. Alexander McQueen chose to show his catwalk collection (Spring/Summer 2010) as a presentation. The use of new technology and social media means that consumers and brands are now ruled by the notion of 'every time, everywhere'.

Design platforms

There are many design platfor[...] designer guild websites that provide independent designers and young emerging designers with the opportunity to become a member and have a platform from which to promote their profile to a wider and often international audience.

<www.acj.org.uk>

The Association for Contemporary Jewellery supports and develops the voice, audience and understanding of contemporary jewellery.

<www.klimt02.net>

Klimt02 showcases news and a wide range of international talent in the contemporary jewellery world.

<www.artjewelryforum.org>

The Art Jewelry Forum (AJF) supports the understanding of contemporary jewellery.

<www.photostore.org.uk>

The Crafts Council's visual database has more than 60,000 images from the UK Crafts Council's Collection, *Crafts* magazine, exhibitions and fairs and a database of around 1,000 contemporary, innovative makers selected by the Crafts Council panel.

<www.whoswhoingoldandsilver.com>

The UK Goldsmiths' Company's website gives members of the public direct access to the workshops of Britain's leading designers of contemporary jewellery, enabling them to source distinctive jewellery and silverware.

<www.craftcouncil.org>

The American Craft Council is a non-profit organization that promotes artisan jewellery makers and trade shows.

E-tailing

Home shopping originated in the 1950s through catalogues and today online retail represents one of the fastest growing platforms for the jewellery market. Online shopping offers the customer a wealth of merchandise across all brands and price levels.

At the upper echelons of the market, Net-a-Porter sells pieces from international brands and new talent; Astley Clarke supplies specifically to customers looking for fine jewellery, while Bottica caters for the fashion jewellery market.

Young designers are benefitting from new 'marketplace' websites. These online stores retail a large number of designers and unlock the great potential of what was once a fragmented marketplace. They offer the customer a one-stop destination for new talent and products that provide an alternative to the run-of-the-mill, mass-produced and impersonal, which is increasingly appealing in a sophisticated age. Fledgling designers benefit by having ready access to global consumers from the start and do not have to invest significantly in large quantities of stock.

Buyers

Established brands have their own route to market via standalone stores, concessions in airports and department stores, pop-up shops and online stores. Smaller brands and individual designers can generate sales independently via trade events such as Première Class, Paris, New York International Gift Fair and London Fashion Week. Such events are useful for designers since they provide an opportunity to get instant feedback on their collections from buyers from global department stores, boutiques and customers.

17. Bottica is an online marketplace selling unique jewellery and fashion accessories by emerging designers from around the world.

18. EG Studio is an online website selling jewellery from a range of designers, as well as bespoke and bridal jewellery and accessories.

17

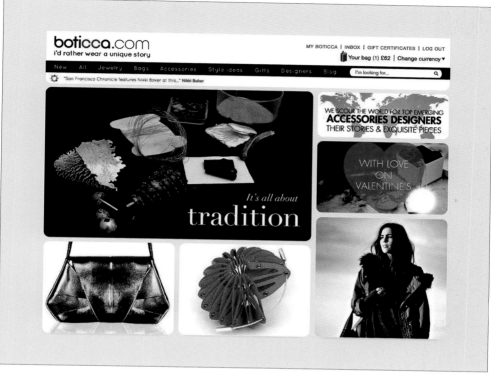

18

Juliet Rowe has combined a lifelong passion for jewellery with a career as a PR consultant and has worked with some fine jewellery brands.

19. 'Diamond cage' stud earrings made with 18ct gold plate and set with diamonds by Lestie Lee.

20. Handmade 'Cecilia' silk scarf featuring a Russian doll design by Age of Reason for Coco de Mer.

Juliet Rowe started her PR career in an agency and is now an independent consultant. She says: 'I'm armed with the ability to combine all roles into one; working on admin and reports, press releases, placing features, organizing events, attending trade shows, organizing shoots and send-outs.'

When starting out in this competitive – and very small – luxury world, it takes time to get noticed and earn respect. The most invaluable experience has to be understanding the pressures of retail, the politics on the shop floor and how to deal with the end customer.

The PR industry can be a frustrating and fickle business: a designer is in one day and out the next. The market is saturated and the competition is immense. PRs from big and small brands are contacting the same handful of journalists.

When times are difficult, often it is the PR who takes the flack, including during economic downtimes. When the client loves the collection but the PR might think otherwise, knowing that it will be difficult to get decent editorial, it can be stressful.

Juliet advises it is not all 'Absolutely Fabulous'! Not just champagne and parties; you have to appreciate the industry, understand the process from the bench in the workshop, to the windows in the store. There is a lot of administration involved in putting on an event, so much behind-the-scenes activity. The worst aspect of all, is hosting a press event and the press not turning up.

Don't take it personally when your product has not been featured even if you personally transported the jewellery to the shoot. Or when you rushed to the newsagents to buy the magazine in which you hoped that your product was being promoted only to find no mention at all. The editor has the last say and often, the picture editor has had to do a lot of last-minute cutting.

20

To create a lookbook you should begin by researching the overall look you are trying to achieve. A good starting point is to gather a variety of press clippings from magazines – such as *Vogue*, *Pop*, and *Vogue Italia* – that feature the best photographers, make-up artists and stylists, as well as campaigns from the best jewellery brands.

Each campaign or editorial image has been painstakingly constructed, styled, lit and photographed and conveys a dynamic image. The emphasis is on drawing the viewer's eye towards the piece of jewellery and background colours that are most sympathetic to the metal and stone colour, volume and proportions of a piece. The model and the clothing used in the image may be quirky, classical or edgy, depending on the theme of the collection and the brand story.

- Study how brands and in-store merchandisers display their accessories and jewellery. To help you to better understand how brands are built, pay attention to composition, scale, and use of colour and still-life installation. Having begun to research how styled images are configured, you will be better prepared to create your own story and brand vision.

- Look at popular style blogs and magazines for inspiration. Choose elements of their layouts and typography that you find eye-catching and use these as a basis for designing your own lookbook.

- Collect catalogues from jewellery brands that you admire and study how they set out their products for maximum impact, and look at their use of branding.

- If you are creating a hard copy of your lookbook, consider printing your price list on a separate sheet that can be inserted into the back of the document – in this way the prices can be easily updated if bullion costs change without having to reprint the entire lookbook.

- List both your wholesale and recommended retail prices and if you are approaching overseas buyers, ensure that your price lists are listed in the relevant currency.

21. SMITH/GREY have included their portraits – Birgit Marie Schmidt (SMITH) and Sofus Graae (GREY) – in their lookbook.

22. SMITH/GREY show their work tools as part of their publicity material. These images reflect their distinctive brand story, where even the design process is marketed beautifully.

Marketing

21

22

Opiom Velourosa Purpra
necklace, made with lacquered
silver, white gold, rubies, diamonds
and rhyolite, designed by Victoire
de Castellane.

The jewellery industry is highly competitive, the most successful and iconic designers are those whose designs transcend trends, themes and influences, and strike a balance between being innovative and being commercially sound.

In this chapter, we look at the various aspects of a designer's career and in particular at design collaborations and consultancy.

The industry has many different aspects in which a designer may be involved, whether working for a brand or in the running of their own creative practice. Formal training is not a prerequisite to entering into a career in jewellery design, unless your intention is to work for an established commercial brand, in which case it is essential.

A good starting point for those without any prior experience of the industry is to undertake a foundation course in the following: jewellery design, CAD, jewellery making and gemology. These courses will give you a taste of the subject before you decide whether you wish to commit to a full-time BA Honours degree. Following a degree course, some people may undertake a postgraduate course, such as an MA in Jewellery Design and some postgraduates (graduates in North America) may go on to do a PhD.

Apprenticeships are less common than they once were and comprise a lengthy duration of practical study with a master craftsman; these have been largely replaced with university supported work placements or internships with brands or established independent designers and makers. Influential programmes and schemes in the UK include the Goldsmiths' Centre, set up by the Goldsmiths' Company, close to Hatton Garden, the traditional home of the trade in London. The Centre provides postgraduate education, business skills tuition and support for young goldsmiths, and teaches craft skills to pre-apprentice silversmiths. It also has business start-up studios.

Today, many budding jewellery designers enter the field from other sectors such as banking, marketing or modelling. Most industry experts and opinion-formers will agree that there is no substitute for formal training of some sort.

1

1. The 'Nightshade' necklace was designed by Jess Mackinnon. Initially self-taught, Jess then trained at two of the UK's most respected jewellery schools to hone her skills in precious metals and jewellery design.

Internships and networking

One route into the jewellery industry is to undertake a work placement. This is an excellent way to build an understanding of what it is like to work in a commercial environment. Students can pick up practical tips, learn from experienced designers and see how the design cycle works. You will meet people who may be able to help you with your career and introduce you to other industry experts who may provide other valuable opportunities.

The first step is to find a company willing to offer a work placement since competition amongst students, or even those with previous experience, is fierce, so graduates need to be persistent. Work placements are often unpaid or only reimburse travel expenses. When you start, you will be working because you have a passion for what you do. Many tutors and those more experienced will tell you that the first five years of a jewellery designer's career are the hardest, but if you persevere you will find it is a fantastically creative and close-knit industry in which to work.

Many established brands run design competitions and awards as part of a college course or university curriculum. These opportunities are vital in boosting a student's CV and afford them the possibility of connecting directly with a brand. If a student is fortunate enough to create a winning design, this often puts them in a good position when applying for a work placement. Winners of design competitions usually receive a financial prize, samples of the product and in some cases a design fee. They also see their designs put into production and sold in the brand's stores.

Networking skills, an element of luck and determination will affect how successful you are likely to be. You can meet like-minded people at exhibitions, fashion shows, parties and lectures. Taking a part-time role on the shop floor of a brand is another alternative to working your way up the career ladder, while studying design. It also provides you with direct experience of dealing with the end consumer, which is invaluable to understanding what the barriers may be to achieving sales. Always be approachable, listen and take direction from experienced people, since employers will assess both your talent and communication skills in equal measure.

You can also be proactive by utilizing networking and social media to connect with individuals or groups. LinkedIn and Luxury Society are good professional networks and social media community platforms, such as Tumblr, Stylehive, Kaboodle, Polyvore, Facebook, Google Circles and Twitter, are useful for self-promotion. Visiting trade fairs and networking is very important since cold calling and sending unsolicited CVs/résumés is often unlikely to engender a positive response from potential employers or buyers. However, it is worth being proactive and contacting designers to find out if they have internships available.

2. 'Handcuffed Bear' necklace made with 18ct gold-plated sterling silver from Momocreatura's 'Nearly Dead' collection. The designer Momoko Tamura creates pieces more akin to 3D illustration or wearable sculpture. Her influences are drawn from the conflict between Japanese heritage and European culture, old and modern, and her childhood curiosities, as well as exploring the boundaries between fantasy and reality.

2

The term 'contemporary designer' is used to denote a group of young, less internationally available independent designers whose collections are usually sold through fashion stores such as Browns and Dover Street Market in London, Loveless in Tokyo, Colette in Paris, Jeffrey in New York and Corso Como in Milan. Many are involved in collaborations with global brands or fashion designers as well as running their own creative practices.

Many collections made by less-established jewellery designers are often favoured by the press, due to their creative outrageousness, which is an antidote to more established designers that have been heavily covered by the media. An independent designer may want to be represented by a PR agent who will secure press coverage for a fee.

Lifestyle

It can be very demanding and often financially unstable being a new independent designer; there is no fixed income and no holiday or sick pay. Investing in stock can be difficult unless you secure an investor or backer. You need to be able to turn your hand not just to designing, but also to areas such as finance, selling and marketing; and it can, at times, feel isolated. On the plus side, working independently gives you creative free rein, and the opportunity to work on different projects at a pace that suits your temperament.

The most successful independent designers often work as part of a team, with the business partner lending complementary expertise, such as strong financial business or marketing acumen. Surrounding yourself with mentors and advisors is also a means of gaining invaluable support.

Schemes and awards

There are many awards and sponsored schemes designed to assist young designers in establishing themselves professionally; including financial sponsorships, mentoring, sponsored exhibitions and work placements.

New Generation (NEWGEN)

The British Fashion Council created NEWGEN to identify, promote and mentor talented new designers. The scheme, supported by Topshop, offers designers sponsored presentation or exhibition space to display their collections.

Walpole's Crafted Programme

Arts & Business and Walpole jointly founded Walpole's Crafted Programme, which is a non-profit-making organization that furthers the interests of the British luxury industry. It provides mentoring and business advice to young, craft-based entrepreneurs each year.

British Crafts Council Awards

The British Crafts Council runs a number of awards including the One Year On exhibition for recent graduates and Creative Industries BootCamp an intensive five-day workshop for creative graduates and start-up companies.

KickStart Programme

The KickStart Programme offers a commercial launch pad to young designers to exhibit at International Jewellery London.

The Prince's Trust

The Prince's Trust Enterprise Programme and Development Awards supports young people aged 13–30.

Goldsmiths' Craft & Design Council

In the UK, Goldsmiths' Craft & Design Council's awards are designed to promote excellence among those engaged in the silversmithing and the jewellery trade.

New Designers Award

New Designers at the Business Design Centre supports new UK emerging talent and creativity with an industry award that has a direct impact on the careers of the winners.

International Talent Support (ITS)

ITS is an organization that acts as a bridge between fashion schools and the fashion industry. It holds competitions that are open to jewellery students and young jewellery designers worldwide.

American Jewelry Design Council New Talent Competition

AJDC holds an annual contest to find an outstanding new talent in fine jewellery.

Training > Contemporary designer > Case study: Brand designer

Brand designer

Many designers starting out will opt for the financial stability of working for an established brand, which affords the opportunity to learn the commercial aspects of design within a more experienced team and to visit suppliers and factories. Depending on design style and experience, a designer will usually spend his or her career dedicated to a specialist market such as fine, fashion or commercial jewellery; although it is not unheard of for a designer to move from fashion to fine jewellery.

3

The flip side of this is that a designer is required to balance their own personal creative identity with the needs and the profile of the brand, which ultimately comes first.

Brand designers' careers may span junior designer, senior designer, to head of design and finally the most talented may achieve the position of creative director. The brand designer will have the opportunity to be involved with many aspects of the brand, either directly or indirectly, and seeing your products sold internationally in stores is very rewarding.

3. 'Frog' ring from the fine jewellery brand Boodles.

4. 'Flamingo' ring by Guy Robertson a brand designer with Boodles.

A Career in Jewellery

Guy Robertson

Guy Robertson graduated from Central Saint Martins, London, UK, in 2007. He won the Bright Young Gems initiative at International Jewellery London (IJL) and worked as a freelance designer as well as designing his own collections for six months.

Following this, Guy worked for Links of London as a junior designer. While at Central Saint Martins his designs were selected as part of a competition run by Links of London and were subsequently produced and sold in their stores.

Guy joined Boodles in 2009 as a brand designer. He says: 'When working for a brand, you always have to be respectful of the brand's style and immerse yourself in and love that style. I think it is important to try to identify a brand that suits you as much as you suit them when applying for jobs'.

When employed by a company you learn that there is so much that goes into making a product, other than just design; you work with PR, marketing, production and workshops. Studying sales figures and how collections perform and then learning how to apply these observations to your designs is also important.

Guy starts the design process by doing lots of research. He works with amazing and rare gemstones at Boodles, which are very inspiring, and coming up with a design that complements a particular stone is very rewarding.

When working with customers on bespoke projects, Guy needs to be aware of the budget, whether there is a particular theme, animal, or source of inspiration the client has a kinship with, or a preference for a specific stone. Through talking to clients, he gets a feel for their lifestyle and then balances this with an appropriate aesthetic.

Guy aims to design pieces that are current but also timeless, which can be handed down through the generations.

4

Many designers consult for established global brands for a fixed one-off fee or retainer. This is sometimes referred to as 'white label' work as the design work is undertaken anonymously. Designers are briefed by the creative director and may work on very specific capsule ranges or technical projects that require their specialist expertise.

Increasingly, designers' roles are becoming more sophisticated. Some have close relationships with fashion designers, from whom they will design each season, influencing and playing a part in the design process and generally a designer acting as a consultant will already have attained a considerable amount of industry experience and knowledge.

5. Atelier Swarovski necklace in white opal by Manik Mercian.

6. Leather poppy brooch designed by Kleshna for the Royal British Legion.

Designer collaborations

Many fashion stores sell specially created jewellery as part of their portfolio. In exchange for the designed range, the retailer arranges the production, sourcing, materials and visual promotion. This arrangement is mutually beneficial and profitable to both parties, since the designer benefits from the association with a major stockist and the retailer benefits from the cachet of working with an innovative, emerging or established designer.

Brands such as Victoria's Secret and mass-market fashion-focused retailers such as Topshop and H&M have identified the value and prestige of promoting guest or celebrity designers to enliven their core ranges. Brands often employ celebrities or celebrity designers for one-off collections.

Collaborative collections are often capsule ranges and may offer cheaper versions of past pieces, allowing a broader customer base to buy into the designer's 'vision'.

Swarovski has pioneered this strategy with Atelier Swarovski, a luxury crystal accessories collection that presents cutting-edge accessories celebrating innovative design from the worlds of fashion, jewellery, architecture, lighting, and stage and screen.

5

Corporate projects

Many large, established brands design and supply ranges or individual products to corporate clients such as banks, airlines and beauty companies. Products are designed to portray a company's image, values and identity. The designer will often work to a very tight budget, and may modify an existing product rather than designing an entirely new item. The company's logo and corporate colours may be incorporated into the design.

Many beauty brands operate consumer 'gift with purchase' or employee 'recognition gifting' and sporting events such as the Olympics can demand the design of medals and trophies. Creating such corporate products can be a highly lucrative revenue stream for a jewellery or silverware company.

Designers may also work with charities to create exclusive products, which are mutually beneficial and raise awareness of the charities' concerns.

6

Case study: Brand designer > **Design consultancy** > Interview: Erickson Beamon

7

8

7. Karen Erickson and Vicki Beamon.

8. Antique gold-plate bracelet made with Swarovski crystals from the Erickson Beamon 'Key Largo' collection (S/S 2012).

Erickson Beamon is an acclaimed international fashion jewellery brand, which was founded in the 1980s by Vicki Beamon and Karen Erickson. The Erickson Beamon clientele includes the First Lady, Michelle Obama, and the British Prime Minister's wife Samantha Cameron as well as pop icons such as Lady Gaga, Beyoncé, and Madonna.

How did the brand start?

KE: Erickson Beamon was born out of necessity. I was designing clothes with a friend. Nobody would loan us jewellery for our show, so we decided to make our own. Vicki came to help me, and Erickson Beamon was born.

VB: When we started out there were very few jewellery designers around so we decided to make pieces ourselves. We made use of our love of craft and began stringing crystals and beads onto suede.

How does your style differ?

KE: Vicki and I are a dynamic duo; we've been partners for so long that we collaborate effortlessly. We exchange ideas and expertise as easily as breathing. Design, for us, is second nature.

VB: After working together all these years we are on a similar wavelength, each season we find a particular mood or trend in the air that informs our pieces.

What is the brand's ethos?

KE: Always be fabulous. Try to have fun. Love life, and design with integrity.

VB: Fashion goes hand-in-hand with Erickson Beamon's aesthetic. We've continued to collaborate with designers throughout our history. Erickson Beamon pieces are both trend led and concept based.

What in your mind makes a good design?

KE: Beauty, grace, and quality.

9

9. Coral and rose gold necklace made with hand-painted stones and Swarovski crystals from the Erickson Beamon 'In the Mood for Love' collection (S/S 2012).

10

10. Crystal and leather mask from the Erickson Beamon 'Night Porter' collection (S/S 2012).

VB: Excellent craftsmanship, the longevity of an item and the comfort of the person wearing a piece are incredibly important factors. Every designer will find a different interpretation on a style or particular era. There is a never-ending flow of ideas and this is what is so glorious about jewellery. There are always new concepts and methods of design, which presents new ways of challenging past design.

Describe the team at Erickson Beamon.

KE: My team is literally a family. In production, we have generations working together (mothers, daughters, and grandmothers). A new team member would be someone with us for less than ten years.

VB: Having such a long-standing and dedicated team is invaluable, I know my ideas can be interpreted and understood as we have been working alongside each other for so many seasons. I feel truly blessed and grateful to be able to come in every day to my studios and workshops and be creative – I'm very fortunate in this respect and it is a great feeling to be doing what you love.

What advice would you give to a young designer trying to become established?

KE: Don't give up. Be prepared to work hard, and don't expect anything.

VB: Personal contacts are invaluable! You must find ways to meet the people at the magazines, call people that you respect and think are fabulous and say you want to work with them! Making personal contact is a vital step, despite all the social networking sites out there.

Nadja Swarovski

11. Nadja Swarovski

12. Atelier Swarovski silvershade cuffs by Mary Katrantzou.

Nadja Swarovski is a member of the executive board of the world's leading crystal brand, which was founded by her great-great-grandfather, Daniel Swarovski in 1895.

Born in Austria in 1970, Nadja was educated in Europe and America and is currently based in London with her husband and three children.

Nadja's career began at Larry Gagosian, one of the world's most powerful and influential gallerists. She went on to work for Eleanor Lambert, the legendary New York fashion PR. This experience, at the heart of the art and fashion worlds, provided an ideal platform from which to initiate a new branch of the family business.

Nadja joined Swarovski in 1995 and set about implementing a series of visionary initiatives which have transformed the company's image, turning crystal into a much desired component in the creative industries, used at the forefront of designer trends.

Forging relationships across the globe, Nadja has challenged established and emerging designers in fashion, jewellery, design, lighting and stage and screen – including Alexander McQueen, Zaha Hadid, Tord Boontje, Karl Lagerfeld, Ron Arad and Mary Katrantzou – to push the boundaries of crystal use in new and revolutionary ways.

Swarovski Runway Rocks

What was the impetus for Swarovski Runway Rocks?

There are two core business groups within Swarovski. The first is the consumer goods division where products are sold within our global retail stores and the second is the business-to-business side, which supplies crystals to the fashion, jewellery and the lighting industries.

13

14

13. Atelier Swarovski large double cuffs and ring by Mary Katrantzou.

14. Atelier Swarovski cuffs by Mary Katrantzou.

For many years, Swarovski has played an indispensable role in the fashion industry with long-standing creative partnerships with labels such as Chanel, Yves Saint Laurent, and Dior. Our mission was to reintroduce the brand to the world of fashion by collaborating with and providing our product to innovative designers such as the late Alexander McQueen, Philip Treacy, Zac Posen and many others. Engaging designers to work with us creatively had a huge brand and sales impact, so we decided to try the same exercise with jewellery and Swarovski Runway Rocks was born.

We asked emerging designers to create their ultimate catwalk jewel and gave them *carte blanche* in terms of creativity. We launched this jewellery initiative internationally – New York, London, Beijing, Shanghai – and it was amazing to see the many different ways in which crystal could be used on the catwalk and in the field of jewellery design.

We worked closely with the jewellery historian Vivienne Becker on Swarovski Runway Rocks and she introduced us to many wonderful designers.

Why is championing emerging talent important to you?

Swarovski's support and vision started in 1999 when we opened an office in New York and when fashion giants such as Donna Karan, Calvin Klein, and Ralph Lauren were dominating the industry. At that time, new designers did not have a platform for their work and were not showing during New York Fashion Week; not one journalist wrote about young fashion designers.

We thought that was such a great shame and felt we should support them. Now it's all about new designers and supporting their vision financially, while helping them to build their profile. Swarovski provides emerging talent with a platform to help young designers evolve and develop their careers.

15

16

15. Atelier Swarovski rings by Jonathan Saunders.

16. Atelier Swarovski large opal ring by Manik Mercian.

Atelier Swarovski

How do you choose the names you work with for Atelier Swarovski?

Atelier Swarovski was inspired by Anna Wintour (editor-in-chief of American *Vogue*) who felt that there was a disconnect between the Swarovski jewellery in our stores and how the product was being used on the catwalk.

In response to this, the first designers we collaborated with showcased their collections on the catwalk and we also gave them the opportunity to create a jewellery collection to be sold in our stores and other high-end retailers. Designers such as Proenza Schouler, Christopher Kane, and Jonathan Saunders created collections for us that were truly fashion jewellery.

We also worked with various jewellery designers and architects such as Zaha Hadid; Atelier Swarovski became a platform for jewellery expression from artists across various different fields.

Usually Swarovski has an 18-month development process, but for Atelier Swarovski it's reduced to six months in order to cater to the fashion seasons.

We launch twice a year at Paris Fashion Week and then travel the collection internationally.

For Swarovski it represents a fresh and more fashion-driven line. We are educating the Swarovski customer about upcoming designers and the designer is fully credited in our stores. We consider all the designers we work with to be artists and we are so proud of their creativity.

Who are your design heroes?

My true inspiration is the late Alexander McQueen. His style was incredibly unique and his designs projected a very strong femininity that was so appropriate for human evolution, the role of women and the issues that they face.

A Career in Jewellery

17

18

17–18. Atelier Swarovski 'Flame' ring and necklace by Viktor & Rolf.

Alexander's creative and historical references and use of materials were extraordinary; there was so much knowledge behind what he did. Sarah Burton is doing an amazing job stepping into his shoes.

What advice would you give students and young designers?

Believe in yourself and don't be afraid to develop your own style, this in turn creates integrity, which people admire. Market yourself as an individual and an artist, the design world is so competitive and it is an advantage to have a name and a story behind each creation.

Product quality is a major consideration; a quality product helps designers to build a strong reputation and also instils consumer confidence and trust. A quality product is also a sustainable and enduring one.

The younger design generation must ensure a balance between creativity and commercialism if they wish to be successful, creativity alone is not enough.

Projects in your portfolio should tell a story through images, outcomes, drawings, material research and activities. They should be carefully selected and relate to specific finished pieces. Your portfolio should show the sources, research and development materials pertaining to the six to eights projects that you have chosen. Your portfolio should also include a mission statement giving a concise overview of your design approach and inspirations as a designer.

Presentation tips

Your portfolio must be well presented. Ensure that you have omitted blank or messy pages and check for glue marks, torn pages, and smears on plastic sleeves. Check that all spelling is correct on titles, logos and in the text. Clients and recruitment agencies do notice these things, so double checking everything will pay dividends and gives you the best possible chance of progressing to that final interview.

Practice presenting your portfolio and write yourself a checklist and a set of explanatory notes, so that you are clear and confident in your own mind. You can then use this to ensure you are not missing any information. Remember that you may not always be present when your portfolio is being reviewed, so you should be certain that the layout and work presented is self-explanatory and samples are clearly labelled.

CV/résumé

A CV/résumé should be no more than two pages, detailing your most recent employment or placement first. It must also include details of your education and training and any awards that you have received. It should be easily digestible for a potential employer or recruiter. Main headings should state the title and dates of the position or placement you held followed by bullet points listing your key achievements and responsibilities in the role.

In the case of applying directly to a brand, you should enclose a covering letter – this should be succinct and demonstrate that you have made yourself familiar with the company's background and details of the role for which you are applying. It should include your contact details and salary expectations.

Should you be successful in gaining an interview, be positive when presenting your work. Do your homework so that you feel confident that you have learned all you can about your potential employers, their customers, design ethos and product portfolio.

If appropriate, do a comparative shop (store visit), it is time well spent. If you can create a sample design project tailored to the company, this will demonstrate you are enthusiastic, knowledgeable and resourceful.

Jewellery is a vibrant and exciting industry in which to work. We have taken you on an introductory journey through the history of jewellery and the many facets of design and production, introducing you to some of the industry's leading players and new, emerging talent.

It is clear that technology and material advances are redefining the industry, while jewellery continues to be a testament to our emotions and a means of conveying our stories and ideas in a tangible way. It is important to test boundaries, express ideas confidently and share your imagination with others.

Naturally, it has only been possible to share a select number of designers and brands in this book, alongside the work of several talented students, but their work offers a unique insight into creative practice today, offering a stimulating taste of what you may expect should you choose to explore the subject further.

19

19. 'Tarsier' skull ring made with silver and rose-gold-plated and set with a pink topaz stone, from Violet Darkling.

Interview: Nadja Swarovski > **Portfolio and CV presentation** > Conclusion

Anticlastic raising
A technique of metal forming, where sheet metal is formed directly with a hammer on a sinusodial (snake-like) stake. A flat sheet of metal is shaped by compressing its edges and stretching the centre so that the surface develops two curves at right angles to each other.

Bijoutiers
A French term for jewellers who work with inexpensive materials.

Brand DNA
Refers to a brand's visual identity which is composed of colours, emotive phrases, logos and iconic products.

Bricolage
A construction made of whatever materials are at hand; something created from a variety of available things.

CAD
Computer-aided design refers to any piece of software that can be used to design on a computer.

Comp shop
The comparison of competitors' stock in terms of material, price and style, which can be conducted in store or on online.

Costing
The estimated price of producing a product.

Critical path
A document that plots key deadlines in the design and manufacturing process.

Ductility
A metal's ability to be drawn, stretched, or formed without breaking.

Forecasting
The process of predicting forthcoming trends.

Hero product
A distinctive product that is representative of the essence of a collection's style, and one that has the potential to become iconic over time.

Joailliers
A French term for jewellers who work with expensive materials.

Lookbook
Used for press, buyers and customers, a lookbook showcases a collection in a catalogue style format.

Memento mori jewellery
Jewellery designed specifically to commemorate the deceased.

Mokume gane
Mokume gane is a mixed-metal laminate with distinctive layered patterns, first made in seventeenth-century Japan.

Moodboard
The compilation of research materials, images and references grouped together to visually communicate ideas.

Pack shot
A catalogue-style image of a product on a white background used in a lookbook, or supplied to retailers and press.

Pavé
A French term meaning 'paved', it is used to describe setting of precious stones placed so closely together that no metal shows.

Prototype
The first version of a product or a sample of a design created before the final manufacture of a collection.

Range plan
A document detailing the number of products and price points in a collection alongside associated market research.

Bibliography

Adams, Maia
Fashion Jewellery
Catwalk & Couture
Laurence King Publishing (2010)

Church, Rachel
Rings
V&A Publishing (2009)

De Lomme, Maureen
Mourning Art & Jewellery
A Schiffer Art Book (2004)

Duquette, Tony and Wilson, Hutton
Jewellery
Abrams (2011)

Estrada, Nicolas
New Rings 500 + Designs
from around the World
Thames & Hudson (2011)

Hemachandra, Ray and Le Van, Marthe
Master Gold Major Works
by Leading Artists
Lark Publishing (2009)

Müller, Florence
Costume Jewellery for Haute Couture
Thames & Hudson (2006)

Peacock, John
20th Century Jewelry
Thames & Hudson (2002)

Peltason, Ruth
Jewelry from Nature
Thames & Hudson (2010)

Phillips, Clare
Jewels & Jewellery
V&A Publishing (2008)

Various authors
The Art of Silver Jewellery
Skira (2006)

Venet, Diane
The Artist as Jeweller
Skira (2011)

Woolton, Carol
Fashion for Jewels
100 years of Styles & Icons
Prestel (2010)

Woolton, Carol
Drawing Jewels for Fashion
Prestel (2011)

Young, Anastasia
The Workbench Guide to Jewelry
Techniques
Thames & Hudson (2010)

500 Gemstone Jewels
Lark Books (2010)

Awards and schemes

www.craftanddesigncouncil.org.uk
http://crafteduk.org
www.craftscouncil.org.uk
www.designinnovationawards.co.uk
http://ftape.com
www.jewellerylondon.com
www.klimt02.net/awards/new-traditional-jewellery-2012-design-contest
www.klimt02.net/fairs/schmuck-2012
www.klimt02.net/awards/talente-2012-competition
www.ktponline.org.uk
www.londonfashionweek.co.uk
www.newdesigners.com
www.princes-trust.org.uk
www.ukjewelleryawards.co.uk

Jewellery associations & guilds

Association for Contemporary Jewellery
www.acj.org.uk
British Crafts Council
www.craftscouncil.com
British Jewellers Association
www.bja.org.uk
Cockpit Arts (London, UK)
www.cockpitarts.com
The Goldsmiths Company (London, UK)
www.thegoldsmiths.co.uk
Jewelers of America
www.jewelers.org

Trade shows

BASELWORLD, Basel, Switzerland
Biennale des Antiquaries, Paris, France
Hong Kong Gift Fair, Hong Kong, China
Inhorgenta, Germany
International Jewellery, London, UK
JCK Vegas, Las Vegas, US
ModAmont, Paris, France
New York Gift Fair, US
Première Classe, Paris, France
Sieraad Art Fair, Amsterdam, Holland
Spring Fair, Birmingham, UK

Top Drawer, London, UK
Treasure Exhibition: London Jewellery
Week, UK
Vicenza, Italy

Ethical jewellery

The Alliance for Responsible Mining (ARM):
www.communitymining.org
OroVerde: www.greengold-oroverde.org
www.gold.org
www.kimberleyprocess.com
www.worlddiamondcouncil.com

Jewellery blogs and websites

www.adornlondon.com
www.artjewelryforum.org
www.goldinspirations.com
www.jewellerynewsnetwork.com
www.jewelleryoutlook.com
www.klimt02.net
www.photostore.org.uk
www.professionaljewellermagazine.com
www.retailjeweller.com
www.thejeweller.com
www.thejewelleryeditor.com
www.vogue.fr/joaillerie
www.whosewhoingoldandsilver.com

Social media platforms & networks

www.facebook.com
www.fashionlista.com
www.foursquare.com
www.googlecircles.com
www.linkedin.com
www.luxurysociety.com
www.kaboodle.com
www.polyvore.com
www.stumbleupon.com
www.stylehive.com
www.thefancy.com
www.tumblr.com
www.twitter.com

Online retailers
www.astleyclarke.com
www.bottica.com
www.elizabethgaltonstudio.com
www.etsy.com
www.luisaviaroma.com
www.netaporter.com
www.notjustalabel.com

Jewellery boutiques
Alexis Bittar, New York, US
Econe, London, UK
Fragments, New York, US
Johnny Rocket, London, UK
Kabiri, London, UK
Podium, Paris, France

Concept stores
Atelier, New York, US
Baby Buddha, Paris, France
Bacci's, Vancouver, Canada
Browns, London, UK
Colette, Paris, France
Elements, Chicago, US
Ellhaus, New York, US
Esencial, Sao Paulo, Brazil
Forty Five Ten, Dallas, US
Isetan, Japan
Jeffrey, New York, US
KJ's Laundry, London, UK
Louis, Boston, US
Loveless, Japan
Merci, Paris, France
Moss NY, New York, US
OC Concept Store, New York, US
Start, London, UK
Surface to Air, Paris, France
The Wonder Room, Selfridges,
London, UK

Acknowledgements

I would like to thank all the contributors, creative practitioners, friends and acquaintances who have so generously and willingly agreed to include examples of their work in this book. Thank you for your kind co-operation and open-handedness.

I would like to extend particular thanks to Jack Meyer at Holts Academy for the information kindly provided on the subject of CAD/CAM and to Juliet Rowe for securing the kind co-operation of the formidable House of Lalique, who were after all one of the original pioneers of the jewellery movement.

In alphabetical order, I would like to especially thank all my interviewees for their professionalism and generous spirit; Lara Bohinc, Karen Erickson and Vicki Beamon, Theo Fennell, Maeve Gillies, Katie Hillier, Anne Kazuro-Guionnet, Shaun Leane, Nathalie Mallet, Kasia Piechocka, Dorothée Pugnet, Guy Robertson, Chris Tague, and Stephen Webster.

Special thanks also to Stephen Bottomley at Edinburgh University for access to his talented roster of students and professional perspective. A personal thank you to Professor Simon Fraser, Professor David Watkins, Andrew Marshall and Jan Springer for their pivotal influence in my own career and without whom I would not have been in the position to write this book.

I would also like to thank all of the young, talented designers who continue to refresh and push the boundaries of this art form and without whom this book would not have been possible.

Additional thanks to Stephen Webster, Shaun Leane, Nadja Swarovski and Theo Fennell who continue to be an inspiration both to me and to the industry as a whole.

Finally a special thank you to my editor Kate Duffy for her tireless help and guidance. It has been a pleasure working on this exciting publication, which I hope will inspire a new generation of design talent.

The publishers would like to thank Stephen Bottomley and Karen Bachmann.

Picture credits

Cover: Hanover Saffron; p. 002 Courtesy of Gagosian Gallery; p. 006 Børg Jewellery 2012; p. 009 Mark Large/Daily Mail/Rex Features; p. 010 Institute of Chicago, Guillaume Blanchard; p. 011 africa924/Shutterstock.com, catwalking.com; p. 012 Zzvet/Shutterstock.com, Børg Jewellery 2012, Chris Moore; p. 014 © Deakins & Francis 2011, Mawi; p. 015 Ana de Costa, Hanover Saffron; p. 016 Rex Features, The Art Archive/Museum of London; p. 017 Gisèle Ganne, Jacqueline Cullen; pp. 018–19 Courtesy of Lalique; p. 020 © Cheltenham Art Gallery & Museums, Gloucs, UK/The Bridgeman Art Library; p. 021 Paramount/Kobal/E.R. Richee; p. 022 Sipa Press/Rex Features; p. 023 Hanover Saffron, © Illustrated London News Ltd/Mary Evans; Paramount/Kobal/Howell Conant; p. 024 Sjaak Ramakers; p. 025 © Condé Nast Archive/Corbis; p. 026 Gunter W. Kienitz/Rex Features; p. 027 Gisèle Ganne; p. 028 Tomasz Donocik; p. 029 Full Focus Photography Ltd; pp. 030–1 Courtesy of Lalique; p. 032 Leyla Abdollahi, London; p. 033 Jacob Ehnmark, SMITH/GREY Jewellery Design Studio; p. 034 David Ferrua; p. 036 Boodles; p. 037 SMITH/GREY Jewellery Design Studio; p. 038 Mitchell Sams, Ugo Camera; p. 039 Mitchell Sams, David Ferrua; p. 040 Courtesy of Stephen Webster, courtesy of Gagosian Gallery; p. 041 Courtesy of Gagosian Gallery; p. 042 David Dettmann Photography; p. 043 Courtesy of Atelier Swarovski; p. 044 Hedone Romane; p. 045 Violet Darkling; p. 046 Sølve Sundsbø, Katie Hillier; p. 047 Linda Bujoli, Lara Bohinc International Ltd; p. 048 Agi Kolman@kolman photography; p. 050 Hattie Rickards Jewellery; p. 051 Agi Kolman@kolman photography; p. 054 Courtesy of Professional Jeweller, courtesy of Stephen Webster; pp. 055–7 Courtesy of Stephen Webster; p. 058 Elizabeth Campbell, Edinburgh College of Art, Jewellery and Silversmithing Department; Mari Ebbitt, eca 2010; p. 059 Rebecca Vigers, eca, 2010; p. 061 willhayman.com; p. 062 Tim Brightmore; p. 063 Courtesy of Shaun Leane; p. 064 ModAmont © Carol Desheulles, BASELWORLD; pp. 066–7 Lauren Egan-Fowler; p. 069 Lauren Egan-Fowler; p. 070 Dorothée Pugnet; pp. 072–3 Dorothée Pugnet; p. 074 packshot.com, nicholaskayphotography.com; p. 075 Design © Alice Menter 2010, Claire English – Special Jewellery Company; p. 076 Simon Harris, Tim Brightmore; p. 077 Tim Brightmore; p. 079 Tim Brightmore; p. 080 © Ciara Bowles, eca, 2010; p. 083 Mackinnon; p. 084 Courtesy of Erickson Beamon; p. 085 Courtesy of Erickson Beamon, Ken Towner/Evening Standard/Rex Features; pp. 086–8 Sarah Ho; p. 089 Courtesy of Lalique; Ana de Costa; p. 090 Daisuke Sakaguchi, Courtesy of Lalique; p. 091 Courtesy of Lalique; pp. 093–4 Courtesy of Jack Meyer/H3-D Technology Ltd; p. 095 Özer Öner/Shutterstock.com; p. 096 Full Focus Photography Ltd; p. 097 Joanna Dahdah; pp. 098–9 Dorothée Pugnet; pp. 100–1 Salima Thakker; pp. 102–3 Courtesy of Maeve Gillies; pp. 104–5 Mariko Sumiko, eca, 2011; pp. 107–8 Courtesy of Peter Pedonomou; p. 110 John Hooper/LBi; p. 112 Angus Taylor, Hanover Saffron; p. 113 Hanover Saffron; p. 114 Adrian Dennis/Rex Features; p. 115 Longmire; p. 116 Boodles; p. 117 Courtesy of Lalique; p. 119 Elizabeth Galton; p. 120 Jocelyn Burton/De Beers; p. 121 Hanover Saffron; p. 122 Dunhill; p. 129 Dan Lecca; p. 131 Elizabeth Galton; p. 134 Andrew Geoghan, image is subject to copyright law, Elizabeth Galton; p. 135 Elizabeth Galton; p. 136 Dominik Pabis/iStockphoto.com, Dunhill; p. 137 Tanuki Photography/iStockphoto.com, Rex Features; p. 138 nicholaskayphotography.com, William Cheshire; p. 139 Allumer, SHO Fine Jewellery; p. 140 Allumer; p. 141 Jochen Braun; p. 142 Nils Jorgensen/Rex Features; p. 145 Boticca.com, Elizabeth Galton; p. 146 www.packshot.com; p. 147 www.capturefactory.co.uk; p. 149 SMITH/GREY Jewellery Design Studio; p. 151 Courtesy of Gagosian Gallery; p. 152 Mackinnon; p. 154 Tatsutoshi Okuda; pp. 156–7 Boodles; p. 159 Courtesy of Atelier Swarovski, Kaylie Mountford; pp. 160–1 Courtesy of Erickson Beamon; p. 162 Brian Bowden Smith, Courtesy of Atelier Swarovski; pp. 163–5 Courtesy of Atelier Swarovski; p. 167 Violet Darkling.

Publisher's note

The subject of ethics is not new, yet its consideration within the applied visual arts is perhaps not as prevalent as it might be. Our aim here is to help a new generation of students, educators and practitioners find a methodology for structuring their thoughts and reflections in this vital area.

AVA Publishing hopes that these **Working with ethics** pages provide a platform for consideration and a flexible method for incorporating ethical concerns in the work of educators, students and professionals. Our approach consists of four parts:

The **introduction** is intended to be an accessible snapshot of the ethical landscape, both in terms of historical development and current dominant themes.

The **framework** positions ethical consideration into four areas and poses questions about the practical implications that might occur. Marking your response to each of these questions on the scale shown will allow your reactions to be further explored by comparison.

The **case study** sets out a real project and then poses some ethical questions for further consideration. This is a focus point for a debate rather than a critical analysis so there are no predetermined right or wrong answers.

A selection of **further reading** for you to consider areas of particular interest in more detail.

Ethical: aware-ness/reflect-ion/debate

Introduction

Ethics is a complex subject that interlaces the idea of responsibilities to society with a wide range of considerations relevant to the character and happiness of the individual. It concerns virtues of compassion, loyalty and strength, but also of confidence, imagination, humour and optimism. As introduced in ancient Greek philosophy, the fundamental ethical question is: *what should I do?* How we might pursue a 'good' life not only raises moral concerns about the effects of our actions on others, but also personal concerns about our own integrity.

In modern times the most important and controversial questions in ethics have been the moral ones. With growing populations and improvements in mobility and communications, it is not surprising that considerations about how to structure our lives together on the planet should come to the forefront. For visual artists and communicators, it should be no surprise that these considerations will enter into the creative process.

Some ethical considerations are already enshrined in government laws and regulations or in professional codes of conduct. For example, plagiarism and breaches of confidentiality can be punishable offences. Legislation in various nations makes it unlawful to exclude people with disabilities from accessing information or spaces. The trade of ivory as a material has been banned in many countries. In these cases, a clear line has been drawn under what is unacceptable.

But most ethical matters remain open to debate, among experts and lay-people alike, and in the end we have to make our own choices on the basis of our own guiding principles or values. Is it more ethical to work for a charity than for a commercial company? Is it unethical to create something that others find ugly or offensive?

Specific questions such as these may lead to other questions that are more abstract. For example, is it only effects on humans (and what they care about) that are important, or might effects on the natural world require attention too?

Is promoting ethical consequences justified even when it requires ethical sacrifices along the way? Must there be a single unifying theory of ethics (such as the Utilitarian thesis that the right course of action is always the one that leads to the greatest happiness of the greatest number), or might there always be many different ethical values that pull a person in various directions?

As we enter into ethical debate and engage with these dilemmas on a personal and professional level, we may change our views or change our view of others. The real test though is whether, as we reflect on these matters, we change the way we act as well as the way we think. Socrates, the 'father' of philosophy, proposed that people will naturally do 'good' if they know what is right. But this point might only lead us to yet another question: *how do we know what is right?*

You
What are your ethical beliefs?

Central to everything you do will be your attitude to people and issues around you. For some people, their ethics are an active part of the decisions they make every day as a consumer, a voter or a working professional. Others may think about ethics very little and yet this does not automatically make them unethical. Personal beliefs, lifestyle, politics, nationality, religion, gender, class or education can all influence your ethical viewpoint.

Using the scale, where would you place yourself? What do you take into account to make your decision? Compare results with your friends or colleagues.

Your client
What are your terms?

Working relationships are central to whether ethics can be embedded into a project, and your conduct on a day-to-day basis is a demonstration of your professional ethics. The decision with the biggest impact is whom you choose to work with in the first place. Cigarette companies or arms traders are often-cited examples when talking about where a line might be drawn, but rarely are real situations so extreme. At what point might you turn down a project on ethical grounds and how much does the reality of having to earn a living affect your ability to choose?

Using the scale, where would you place a project? How does this compare to your personal ethical level?

01 02 03 04 05 06 07 08 09 10

01 02 03 04 05 06 07 08 09 10

Your specifications
What are the impacts of your materials?

In relatively recent times, we are learning that many natural materials are in short supply. At the same time, we are increasingly aware that some man-made materials can have harmful, long-term effects on people or the planet. How much do you know about the materials that you use? Do you know where they come from, how far they travel and under what conditions they are obtained? When your creation is no longer needed, will it be easy and safe to recycle? Will it disappear without a trace? Are these considerations your responsibility or are they out of your hands?

Using the scale, mark how ethical your material choices are.

Your creation
What is the purpose of your work?

Between you, your colleagues and an agreed brief, what will your creation achieve? What purpose will it have in society and will it make a positive contribution? Should your work result in more than commercial success or industry awards? Might your creation help save lives, educate, protect or inspire? Form and function are two established aspects of judging a creation, but there is little consensus on the obligations of visual artists and communicators toward society, or the role they might have in solving social or environmental problems. If you want recognition for being the creator, how responsible are you for what you create and where might that responsibility end?

Using the scale, mark how ethical the purpose of your work is.

01 02 03 04 05 06 07 08 09 10

01 02 03 04 05 06 07 08 09 10

Working with ethics

One aspect of fashion design that raises an ethical dilemma is the way that clothes production has changed in terms of the speed of delivery of products and the now international chain of suppliers. 'Fast fashion' gives shoppers the latest styles sometimes just weeks after they first appeared on the catwalk, at prices that mean they can wear an outfit once or twice and then replace it. Due to lower labour costs in poorer countries, the vast majority of Western clothes are made in Asia, Africa, South America or Eastern Europe in potentially hostile and sometimes inhumane working conditions. It can be common for one piece of clothing to be made up of components from five or more countries, often thousands of miles apart, before they end up in the high-street store. How much responsibility should a fashion designer have in this situation if manufacture is controlled by retailers and demand is driven by consumers? Even if designers wish to minimise the social impact of fashion, what might they most usefully do?

Traditional Hawaiian feather capes (called *'Ahu'ula*) were made from thousands of tiny bird feathers and were an essential part of aristocratic regalia. Initially they were red (*'Ahu'ula* literally means 'red garment') but yellow feathers, being especially rare, became more highly prized and were introduced to the patterning.

The significance of the patterns, as well as their exact age or place of manufacture is largely unknown, despite great interest in their provenance in more recent times. Hawaii was visited in 1778 by English explorer Captain James Cook and feather capes were amongst the objects taken back to Britain.

The basic patterns are thought to reflect gods or ancestral spirits, family connections and an individual's rank or position in society. The base layer for these garments is a fibre net, with the surface made up of bundles of feathers tied to the net in overlapping rows. Red feathers came from the *'i'iwi* or the *'apapane*. Yellow feathers came from a black bird with yellow tufts under each wing called *'oo'oo*, or a *mamo* with yellow feathers above and below the tail.

Thousands of feathers were used to make a single cape for a high chief (the feather cape of King Kamehameha the Great is said to have been made from the feathers of around 80,000 birds). Only the highest-ranking chiefs had the resources to acquire enough feathers for a full-length cape, whereas most chiefs wore shorter ones which came to the elbow.

The demand for these feathers was so great that they acquired commercial value and provided a full-time job for professional feather-hunters. These fowlers studied the birds and caught them with nets or with bird lime smeared on branches. As both the *'i'iwi* and *'apapane* were covered with red feathers, the birds were killed and skinned. Other birds were captured at the beginning of the moulting season, when the yellow display feathers were loose and easily removed without damaging the birds.

The royal family of Hawaii eventually abandoned the feather cape as the regalia of rank in favour of military and naval uniforms decorated with braid and gold. The *'oo'oo* and the *mamo* became extinct through the destruction of their forest feeding grounds and imported bird diseases. Silver and gold replaced red and yellow feathers as traded currency and the manufacture of feather capes became a largely forgotten art.

Is it more ethical to create clothing for the masses rather than for a few high-ranking individuals?

Is it unethical to kill animals to make garments?

Would you design and make a feather cape?

Fashion is a form of ugliness so intolerable that we have to alter it every six months.

Oscar Wilde

AIGA
Design Business and Ethics
2007, AIGA

Eaton, Marcia Muelder
Aesthetics and the Good Life
1989, Associated University Press

Ellison, David
Ethics and Aesthetics in European Modernist Literature:
From the Sublime to the Uncanny
2001, Cambridge University Press

Fenner, David E W (Ed)
Ethics and the Arts:
An Anthology
1995, Garland Reference Library of Social Science

Gini, Al and Marcoux, Alexei M
Case Studies in Business Ethics
2005, Prentice Hall

McDonough, William and Braungart, Michael
Cradle to Cradle:
Remaking the Way We Make Things
2002, North Point Press

Papanek, Victor
Design for the Real World:
Making to Measure
1972, Thames & Hudson

United Nations Global Compact
The Ten Principles
www.unglobalcompact.org/AboutTheGC/TheTenPrinciples/index.html